Views from the Home Office Window

On Motherhood, Family and Life

Ellen Blum Barish

Debbie:
To the journey that
is motherhood,
may it provide you
with many
gifts!

Best,
Ellen
Blum
Barish

Adams Street Publishing Co.

Versions of the essays in this book were published in *Toledo Area Parent News* and *Ann Arbor Family Press* between 1996 and 2006. "Best Friends" and "What I've Learned from People Without Children" appeared in the *Chicago Tribune* and were syndicated by Tribune Media Services International. "Money in Sight" was aired as a radio commentary on WBEZ-Chicago Public Radio. "Whose Life" can be found on www.writingwoman.com as "The Relative Nature of Writing." Sections from *How to Win Friends and Influence People* by Dale Carnegie in "A Mother's Mark" were excerpted with permission. Statistics reported in "Blended" were provided by the National Stepfamily Resource Center.

Published by Adams Street Publishing Company
1120 Adams Street
Toledo, Ohio, 43604
(419) 244-9859
Fax (419) 244-9871
www.adamsstreetpublishing.com

Library of Congress Cataloging-in-Publication Data

Barish, Ellen Blum
Views from the Home Office Window:
On Motherhood, Family and Life / Ellen Blum Barish

ISBN-10: 0-9792355-0-2
ISBN-13: 978-0-9792355-0-4

1. Motherhood 2. Women's issues 3. Parenting - psychological
4. Spirituality 5. Essays

Cover images:
"Girl running" © 2007 istockphoto.com and Jean Schweitzer
"Window" and "Laptop" © 2007 JupiterImages Corporation
Interior spot illustrations:
"Ferns and florals" © 2007 JupiterImages Corporation

Book cover and page design by Amy Wheeler/Avalon Project Partners.
Portrait photographs by Suzanne Plunkett.
Family photographs provided by the Barish family.

Original paperback edition. 5 4 3 2 1
Printed and bound in the United States of America

*This book is dedicated
to my daughters,
Emily and Jenny Rose,
who educated me in the
art of motherhood and
changed everything.*

Acknowledgments

Over lunch in a suburban Chicago diner, Rebecca Harris convinced me that it would be possible to edit the Toledo parenting newspaper she co-founded with Collette Jacobs from my Skokie, Illinois home office. It struck me as a very out-of-the-box idea, but the arrangement worked out well, that is until it became clear to us all a year later that the paper would be better steered by a Toledo-based editor. When I left the paper as editor, Becky and Collette offered me a life-changing opportunity: monthly column space to write about women's health topics. I am enormously grateful to Collette for keeping me on as a columnist after Becky moved on to other professional ventures, and thankful for the editors who gave me freedom and editorial support, especially Veronica Hughes.

So many columns grew naturally out of conversations with other mothers — smart and sensitive women on whom I continue to rely for reality checks, emotional support or a safe ear. In the order they came into my life, they are: Alysse Einbender, Marianne Mitchell, Kacky Solley, Adrienne Oleck, Katie Houston, Gail Conway, Judith Matz, Sean Rosemeyer, Julie Anza and Paula Clar.

My deep appreciation goes to Dinah McNichols and Christine Needham, former editors at Tribune Media Services International, who first allowed me to dream of a larger audience through syndication. I am indebted to writer friends Mary Ellen Sullivan, Lee Reilly, Nina Barrett, Deborah Leigh Wood, Susan Spaeth Cherry and Bobbie Scheff for insights on a life devoted to words; to Patricia Sullivan for a close, final read at manuscript stage;

Acknowldegements

Nancy Liskar for sharp-eyed editing and proofreading on layouts; Amy Wheeler for an innovative book design and Penny Hirsch for the title of this book.

I will also be forever moved by the wisdom imparted to me by the remarkable and generous women who will always be several steps ahead in their mothering journeys: Deb Sherer, Barbara Byer, Hyma Levin and Sharyn Reiff and, my mother, Nancy Blum, who has always blessed me with her wise, curious and loving presence.

No writer with children could accomplish much without the right caregivers watching over her children. My daughters have been blessed to have known and loved devoted great-grandparents and grandparents, uncles, aunts, child care providers, sitters, teachers and family friends who have kept them engaged, safe and often, overnight.

Of course, the subject matter would have taken a different turn if it were not for the three people who were central to my transformation into a mother. Multi-layered learning continues to grow out of my relationship with my extraordinary daughters, Emily and Jenny Rose, whom I share with great joy with my husband David, an incisive and patient first reader and incomparable partner in the family business.

January 2007

Table of Contents

Preface

When I was close to completing this book, I found myself in the office of a colleague engaging in what I call working-mother talk. The mother of two very young children, she spoke about how in spite of loving her profession, she is acutely aware of every hour she spends apart from them. How on the days when her oldest child has tantrums from the time she walks in the door until just before bed, she wonders if being away from her children is worth the small fortune it costs in child care. How she struggles with ways to lessen her work pressures while remaining productive at the office and being there for her children.

As I listened to her wrestle aloud with these universal working mother quandaries, memories of my own struggles came rushing back. Her serious tone of voice, her knitted brow, her tired eyes were so familiar. It was as if I were looking at myself 10 years ago. As we talked, I realized I was bearing witness to motherhood at work, because even though she was miles from her children, there wasn't a moment in her day that being a mother wasn't at the forefront of her consciousness.

I've come to understand that mothering isn't only found in diaper changing, bath giving, meal preparing, book reading and open armed hugging but equally present when a woman's children are in the front of her mind. My colleague's face said it all: hers was the face of the behind-the-scenes work of mothering — the human face of quality control — and watching her as she expressed her concerns over these big questions struck me as observing her in the act of mothering.

Our exchange also clarified why I was so determined to put

together this collection of pieces. I realized that all of the grappling, the musing, the pondering and the struggles that went into the individual columns making up this collection was a form of mothering of my own. My writing process mirrors this invisible work of motherhood, the hard work our culture doesn't often see, acknowledge or really appreciate.

While some women work their stuff out by running or talking or sleeping, for me, it is through writing. I am blessed to have 12 column inches and a monthly deadline in which to do so. I accomplished this for many years from what I'll call a home office, even though for most of that time, an office would be a loose term at best.

I started writing these columns in the corner of a condominium dining room, moved into a small section of a mildewy basement with one of those sunken windows that never opens and ended up in a second-story bedroom with a window that actually let in light and air.

With each writing spot, the window was vital for my work. Where there was a window, there was perspective and possibility. For a few precious hours when my children were being watched over or engaged by family members, friends, other mothers, sitters or teachers, a window allowed me a fresh view on my mothering. It allowed me to gaze beyond my temporary working space. And at moments, while looking out at the world, I was the lucky recipient of a few moments of insight.

I relied on the vantage points that those squares provided. Along with a quiet space and a working computer, those glass-filled holes in my domestic space gave me everything I needed during the time I was writing these columns. Thanks to the publishers and editors at Adams Street Publishing, I had great freedom — except for the word count — to delve into the subjects on my mind. In 1995, when I first began writing the columns, my daughters were four and eight and I was desperate to find anything resembling a work–life balance. Back then it seemed that everything gnawed at me for attention and everything got short shrift. But not so long after, there was less gnawing, more available attention to spread and fewer demands from my children in the emergency, physical way.

As I wrote these columns, I suspected that I was not alone in thinking that the behind-the-scenes work of motherhood was potent stuff. While it was often tempting to run from many of the issues that my daughters raised, I ultimately found that facing a blank screen was more fruitful, and even useful to others from time to time. E-mail letters from readers confirmed this and ultimately became the final prompt for me to pull together this collection.

These pieces were written in stolen moments around broken legs and broken hearts, hospital stays and hospital leaves, doctor appointments, run-ins with the local police and interventions — a full range of family dramas that build the tapestry we call family life.

I selected pieces that still ring true, even if they do date back 10 years or so. I wanted only to keep what still hit a nerve with me or had moved someone to sit down and jot me a few lines. Pieces that when I returned to them offered possibilities: some wisdom or insight because, as all mothers know, there are no instructions, blueprints, maps or downloads. We get our perspective from the trenches, or maybe from other mothers' momentarily clear sight-lines from home office windows.

Ellen Blum Barish
December 2006

The Barish family in the fall of 1996.
From left: Ellen, Emily (8), Jenny Rose (5), and David.

1995-1996

Middleground

I had a frightening dream after I had lunch with my friend Sean.

She had been telling me how it felt to be the primary caregiver to her two-year-old and nine-month-old sons as well as her 77-year-old ailing mother. Sean's mother lived in another town and had recently been diagnosed with congestive heart failure and adult-onset diabetes. She was telling me about how at 44, she wasn't merely standing in the center of two generations but felt more like she was paddled between them like a Ping-Pong ball.

There she was, changing Peter's diapers one moment and helping her mother steer insulin needles into the right places in her body the next.

There she was, a few years later, Peter finally potty trained, urging her mother to consider adult diapers.

There she was, angsting over whether to bring her mother to live with her, her husband and her sons or to find a nursing home.

There she was, still in early motherhood, rearranging her notions of balance between being a mother, caregiver and creative person, and lucky to get a shower. Though Sean wasn't complaining, nor did she say it, I was struck by the timing. That in the midst of these early motherhood days, her mother gets sick. Just when Sean could have used her the most.

With our life expectancy increasing, I've read reports that we may spend as many as 15 years caring for our parents. Some say the growing numbers of people caring for two generations is the price we pay for marrying later to launch careers. Others say it's the tax for living longer. In any event, it is a women's issue: more than half of the caregivers in the United States are women.

Not only is it an emotional roller coaster, it can also be

financially devastating. Though Sean's mother's health care was covered by Medicare, and she had savings for moving and nursing home expenses, financially, it wiped her mother out.

But harder for Sean than the dollars spent was the constant drain on a precious resource — time. Somewhere in between being a mom, a wife, paralegal, genealogist, neighborhood activist, Victorian flower gardener, homeowner, dog owner and caregiver is my friend Sean: A woman with lots of abilities and interests which, as with many mothers, lay at the bottom of her to-do list. We agreed that the biggest challenge for a woman in her position is in reminding herself to care for the caregiver.

As for my dream, well, it was pretty unsettling. In it, my mother *and* mother-in-law got sick at the same time and I was somehow the only one who could help. Both lived out of town — though only one does in real life — and I had to drop everything and walk onto two other stages in addition to my own.

What stayed with me the morning after that dream was how women can so suddenly be pulled from our own spotlight into the middle of another drama. It strikes me as a recurring theme in a woman's life. How often we are put in the middle of all kinds of decisions: our careers versus our children; our own health versus our family's health. We fashion a life at high speeds like an air-filled Ping-Pong ball flying from one side to the other.

Sean's sandwiched life, and my dream, tell me that whatever middle ground we find — when the ball finally drops — is temporary.

October 1995

Boundaries

My four-year-old daughter and I have a ritual: As soon as she sees me coming through the glass doors of her preschool classroom, she drops everything and barrels across the room at such force you can practically see the smoke coming out of her little feet. I've got to plant myself firmly on that linoleum to receive her with open arms without being knocked over.

Aside from ranking as one of the most pleasant events of my day — black and blue marks notwithstanding — I've come to see that this emphatic greeting has multi-layered meanings for my daughter.

On one level, it's an immediate method of reestablishing contact with me after a long day of being apart. On another, it is a way for her to find out where she ends and her mother begins. Which is a useful exercise in boundary exploration for us both.

Though it is easy to forget (because we are so responsible for them), our children's bodies are their own. By running at top speed into her mother, Jenny Rose is looking for a sturdy and reliable grownup to help her put on the brakes for that sometimes scary four-year-old power, which is hers. That power is the preschool equivalent to a good, healthy body image.

Children start life with an inborn sense of the greatness of their own bodies: They are born with body self-esteem. Healthy babies come into the world believing that everything is possible, capable and beautiful within the realm of their body. And for the most part, they move into toddlerhood and early childhood with these feelings intact.

Until preadolescence. That's the time when, for girls in particular, a perfectly solid sense of the strength and beauty of one's own body begins to disintegrate from messages that if she were thinner, more sculpted or more puffy-lipped, she'd be more wonderful than she already is.

No mother can predetermine how her daughter is going to respond to growing up in a woman's body. Some girls may revel in its gloriousness. Others may retreat with self-consciousness. Either way, I'm sure preaching will make teenage eyes glaze over. I can promote a good, healthy body image only so far with words; the rest I'll have to do by modeling it.

Which brings me back to her preschool classroom doors. Could colliding into her mother after a long day away help her determine how much space she takes up in the world? Might it be a way that she confirms that she exists — and that her mother does, too?

While I'm certain that I won't get that kind of greeting from her when I pick her up from elementary school, I hope I can reassure her about the wonder of her own body when she's, say, 14.

March 1996

Growing Pains

I am no longer the ingenue in the office.

Working with mostly twenty-somethings — bright and intelligent and energetic twenty-somethings — has set my age alarm off. On Monday mornings around the coffee pot, there are accounts of seamless weekends. My younger colleagues take night classes, exercise at lunchtime, live in the city, report on new restaurants, volunteer at local shelters and party until dawn.

I used to be them.

Even though there aren't that many years between us, I find myself furthering the distance without realizing it. I bond with them by making copies of articles on topics that come up in conversations as my grandfather did for me. When one of them came into the office one cold winter morning without a coat, I heard myself actually ask, Where are your coat and mittens?

Though I hadn't seen it before, about when I began to notice the years between us was just about the time when I first saw the sagging and stretchy parts of my body. How much more tired I appeared at the end of the day than they did as we rode in the elevator to go home.

During this private pity party, my oldest daughter turned eight and I decided to take a day off from work to spend it with her.

We went to an interactive children's museum known for its dress-up-and-see-yourself-on-TV exhibit, lifelike miniature supermarket with carts and plastic food items and educational computer games.

In 10 minutes, she had run through most of the exhibits, pulling levers and pressing buttons without much interest. She looked disappointed.

"I can't do these anymore. Something's not right," she said, scoping the landscape.

I urged her to climb the train car or try on some dress-up clothes. Five more minutes passed and it had become clear that Emily had lost interest in the children's museum.

Plaintively she asked, "Mom, can we go?"

Walking to the car, I suggested that perhaps it wasn't that she couldn't do the activities, but that perhaps she just didn't want to do them. She sighed and said, "I guess I've just grown older."

And a moment later, she added, "It's really kind of sad, isn't it?"

It really *is* kind of sad when what you remember as fun no longer provides you with the same adrenaline. Time passes, your body ages, your memories keep you suspended in time, but you've moved on.

That's when I found myself telling her that while she may have outgrown the children's museum, she wasn't losing something, but gaining something. She would be able to keep her memories of great, past museum visits and also allow room for entirely new experiences somewhere else.

Which was right about the moment that I noticed having children around can be very helpful for an aging parent.

You comfort your eight-year-old about how it isn't the end of the world that she's moved on from the children's museum and you recognize that you might just have given yourself some pretty good advice. I may no longer be the energetic young professional at my office, but I do get a heck of a lot of wisdom imparted to me on my days off. When the passages our kids go through parallel our own, it can melt the years between us and make us feel that as long as we are human, we will always be growing out of one stage and moving on to another.

April 1996

Blended

Being a member of a blended family can certainly add a layer of complication to family life. Especially when it comes to life-cycle events.

Several years ago, when I received the invitation for my father's wife's oldest son's wedding, it was there before my eyes in black italic print on handmade textured paper. Boiled down to the hosts' relationship to me, the invitation said that my father's wife and my father, along with my stepbrother's fiancée's father and stepmother and my stepbrother's fiancée's mother and her stepfather requested the honor of my presence at the marriage of their children.

The wording highlighted how complete strangers can be joined together into family because of divorce, remarriage or death.

A wedding is complex with or without a family being blended, but in the months before the nuptials, I found myself looking at the research on stepfamily life. Social scientists believe that stepfamily members are rich sources of information about the inner workings of family relationships and that the issues these family scenarios raise are common to all families, only more public.

And what a large pool of families to observe. Last I checked, at least half of all Americans will have been a part of a stepfamily at some time in their lives. One in three children currently live in a stepfamily arrangement. According to the U.S. Census Bureau, men and women with children remarry faster than those without children: About 80 percent of divorced men and 75 percent of divorced women remarry within four years after their divorce.

The research also says that divorce itself does not harm children. Parental conflict does. High parental conflict is by far the biggest problem for the children.

Blended

The children of blended families are resilient. These children learn how to be flexible.

My parents separated when I was fully grown and married. Even though I was an adult, it was rough. There were some really challenging moments in the years after my parents divorced. We had to renegotiate our definition of family and absorb new family trees and traditions. Photographs of people I did not recognize were displayed on shelves. New paintings were hung on the walls and unfamiliar art objects sat on fireplace mantels and bedside tables. New foods were in the refrigerator and the Thanksgiving meal had a different menu.

We had to work out some bumps and kinks and because there were no directions, we had to go by feel. But it wasn't long before we began to count on those annual family reunions at the beach and discussions about music and Asia at meals. I realized that I had learned an enormous amount about family dynamics that served me well in family life, as well as in my professional and communal one.

A mother I know, a veteran of blended family life, compared blended family struggles to putting precious rocks together in a blender. "It makes a lot of noise," she said. "The rocks rattle around a whole lot, maybe even knock off a few rough edges." But in the long run, she offered, "each member of the family becomes stronger for having gone through the blending process."

People related by life's unexpected events who make new rituals together and call themselves a family are proof, I think, that down deep, we really all do want to get along. Especially when there's something to celebrate.

December 1996

1997-1998

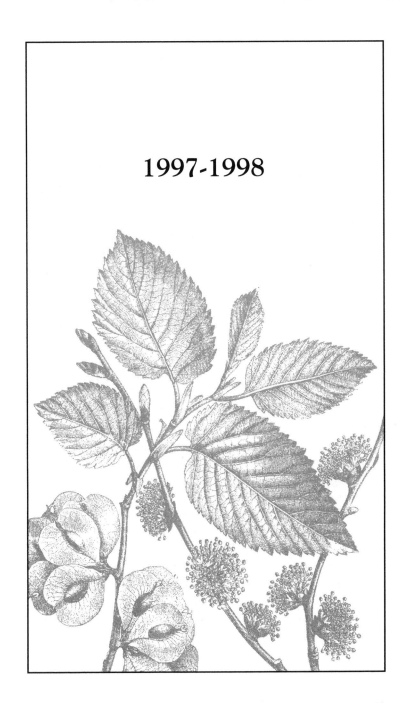

Raising Girls with Voices

I was raised to be a good girl.

A good girl listened well to others and kept how she felt about things, especially if they were contrary, to herself. A good girl didn't offer her opinions or go on about what she thought about people or the world around her. A good girl was considerate of other people's feelings and did not bother others (read: parents).

Growing up this way has provided me with a real dilemma as I raise two daughters. Because I grew up wanting my voice to be heard, I want to make sure that my daughters' voices are acknowledged. But I also want them to be *good girls*.

As my daughters have grown older, these desires have become more at odds. How can I teach them to feel comfortable using their voices while I still carry around the idea that good girls use some *restraint*?

When my daughters were in their early talking years, it was easy to urge them to speak their minds. I'd prod them for their opinions and thoughts about almost everything: *What do you think about this book? These outfits? That movie? How are you feeling about Great Grandpa's death and the outcome of the presidential election?*

And I'd get more answers, opinions and commentaries than a person really wants to hear. Because they are practiced little speakers, my daughters don't often wait to be asked for their opinions. My older daughter gave an unplanned, heartfelt speech to a room full of grownups at a family wedding. My youngest daughter spontaneously called a house full of people to attention and produced an unrehearsed puppet show in which the puppets spoke with gusto about their views of the world. Both of them offer their words generously. And often. About everything.

They are also fountains of information and always ready to share. I've heard more than I could possibly retain about which television actors have crossed over to movies, what schoolmates got new shoes and what color, who the teacher singled out that day, and of course, what they think about all of these events.

Whoever said *Be careful what you wish for because you could actually get it* could use my husband and me as poster parents. Because we weren't going to squash our little girls' voices, we have more running commentary and informational updates than CNN and the local and national newspapers combined. Up until recently, this had struck us as having benefits.

But after long hours of unending expressions of their minds and hearts around our house, in the car, at the grocery store or during a movie, I have begun to think that maybe there is such a thing as being *too* vocal and *too* empowered.

When the voices are continuous, they start to sound like white noise, or worse, Muzak. Speaking for the sake of hearing one's own voice isn't really using one's voice in a very powerful way. Though I had wanted to urge them to speak their minds, I hadn't begun to teach them how they might express themselves *well*.

Recently, I've been sketching my own, more modern, picture of how a young girl can use her voice and be *good* at the same time. The strangest part is, I've concluded, that I don't have to dismiss my own good-girl upbringing. I've come to see it as my next big mothering challenge: I can teach my girls about the balance between being outspoken and considerate of their audience.

First, I need to make them understand that having a voice in the world isn't just about the freedom to speak or about saying whatever is on your mind at the moment. It is also about reflecting first about the meaning of what you want to say — and the timing.

And second, to be truly effective as a speaker, they need to be aware of who is listening. They need to know when they are losing their audience. A little moderation and awareness — some of the attributes of my very own good-girl training — aren't such bad tools. They can be very effective. I need to suggest to them that holding back a little and practicing patience can be a very wise move, something that can make their voices *more* powerful than they already are.

Then we will *really* have a challenge around our house.

May 1997

Triangle

The day my second daughter was born, my family's fate was sealed. We became, in the words of my husband, a *House of Estrogen*.

My husband, a man who grew up with no sisters, joked that we were all going to have to brace ourselves for bathroom brawls, clothing costs and the days when all three of us would be premenstrual at the same time.

While this may come true sooner than we'd like, these events will pale in comparison to what else occurred that day my younger daughter was born. That day a triangle of women was created in our family. You know the triangle I mean: like the one you hated in middle school. The one that one minute felt great to be a part of and the next, left you out like a broken toy. That complex triangle you were simultaneously drawn to but tried to stay away from. And it caught up with me in the privacy of my own home when I was, supposedly, all grown up.

When the triangle is activated, there is no longer a grownup mom and two little girls in the house. Instead there are three little girls all wanting their way and expressing themselves with bravado.

I know that the triangle is present when the little stuff of daily life turns into a competition. When the prevailing motivation is to get more, or just simply, the most. When one of my daughters is sitting in my lap, the other will start trouble, ask for something located in a high-up place or just cry to get me up. Or when my husband and I come home and the sitter insists that she had no problems whatsoever with feeding them dinner, selecting TV shows or putting them to bed. Then I know its possible for life to run smoothly when the third leg of the triangle is out of the house.

Triangle

The triangle is with us is when one of us brings out the arsenal of hurtful words. We are a family of verbal females who know just where to jab. My older daughter knows where the sensitive spots lie for her little sister. My younger daughter is learning her lessons well and flinging them back. They are also well plugged into my mood. They check it out like dogs sniffing for the right tree. Then they try everything from flattery to logic to taking the dishes to the sink (depending on their assessment of my mood) to get what they want.

I am not without my own part in this sharp-angled family geometry. The triangle appears when I've temporarily exchanged my mother role for being one of the girls. If I have had a particularly long day, and one of them is ranting, it is a lethal combination. That's when my role as mother can get confused and the triangle takes shape. Like when my younger daughter asks for ice water for the ninth time and I've just sat down for the first time all day, I sometimes hear myself sounding like one of the girl pack. "Why don't you get it for yourself," I say, in *that* tone.

I am a mother and one-of-the-girls, all rolled into one. But for my daughters, I'm where the buck stops. In the end, I always revert to mother.

Living with such a pointy and angular shape teaches you a few things. Someone is going to get hurt sometimes.

I wish we could emulate less dangerous shapes, like a circle perhaps. Maybe in years to come. For now, it's triangles.

Even if I am one of the girls from time to time, I will always be their mother first.

September 1997

Sex

Sex is very much alive at our house, that is, alive as a topic of conversation. My nine-year-old daughter is asking an awful lot of questions about sexual feelings and development. Questions we knew would come, but so soon?

She wants to know what that feeling is down there when she sits a certain way while I'm steaming broccoli for dinner. She asks about pubic hair and pimples, body odor and bra straps. She wonders aloud when was the first time I had sex, then quickly retracts the question.

While I had been thinking that these questions were a sign of great curiosity and good emotional health, over the last several months I have begun to feel overwhelmed by them. These questions constantly interrupt the flow of other things. When I point out to her that she is probably going through all kinds of hormonal changes, she rails loudly in protest and tears spill everywhere to prove it.

I *am* trying to be patient. I want her to feel understood, heard and not so afraid of all those bodily changes and social pressures.

But lately the questions have come so fast and so furiously, I admit that I haven't been handling them very gracefully. It's distracting to be answering so many questions about sex when I'm trying to fix dinner, drive to a class, put away groceries, pay the bills or get some work done.

I have been short tempered with her. I have given her half answers. I have said, "Let me get back to you on that" and then haven't.

Because I have no more tricks up my sleeves or ideas in my head, I've been reading up on it. Know what I'm finding?

Sex

A child's burgeoning sexuality and maturity can trigger a parent's own crisis.

I've discovered that for many parents, this fast-forward reproductive growth spurt and interest in the subject signal two things: a new phase in their child's life is beginning, and an old phase in the parents' lives is ending.

Which suggests that one's daughter is quickly approaching womanhood. Mothers are likely to long for the past, question the decisions they have made about their lives, and worry about their worthiness and physical appeal.

Could this explain the extra-sensitive way I've been feeling lately? Were these perfectly natural questions forcing me to face my firstborn child's maturation and coming of age? Was I ready to share the grownup woman limelight in the house?

When my daughter wanted to rent the video *Romeo and Juliet*, I resisted for months. Finally, I read the reviews and despite the PG-13 rating, I thought, heck, it's Shakespeare. She's since seen it at least three times. I hadn't been able to figure out what the appeal was for her — all of that Shakespearean English with adult themes of love and death. But I was fascinated to find out that when Romeo and Juliet were courting at age 13, they were considered adults in the eyes of society. Puberty is a modern invention.

This piece of social history encouraged me to take some action. On the recommendation of a friend with an older daughter, I brought home a book about sex with photographs of boys and girls growing older, a discussion of menstruation and tampons and sanitary napkins, an entire chapter about changing feelings and friendships and social life, as well as discussions about sex, pregnancy, hygiene and protection from diseases. My daughter was elated. She scampered to her bedroom and hovered over the book for hours. It stayed in her room for another day or two, but on the third or fourth day she handed it back to me, saying, "Thanks, Mom, but I don't think I'm ready for all of this right now." Neither am I.

October 1997

A Competitive Spirit

My six-year-old daughter *lives* to compete. She thrives on the thrill of the game. She is energized by the effort, stimulated by the score, swept up by the sweat and downright animated by getting the answer. It doesn't matter if it is at the ice rink, on the soccer field or in her kindergarten classroom.

As someone whose idea of competition is that I stay at the same speed on the recumbent bike when I go the gym each week, I was concerned about how her highly ambitious spirit would impact her emotional health.

I fretted that she'd be so into winning that losing would destroy her. I wondered if she'd be so driven to keep her edge that she'd stop learning new things. I worried that going for the trophy would keep her from finding gratification from inside.

Too much of anything — even healthy competition — can be obsessive, even addictive, right? Or just bad news. I'll never forget what Michelle Kwan said in an exit interview after her silver medal win behind Tara Lipinski's gold during the Winter 1998 Olympics. "I got a silver — Mom and Dad — I hope you still love me."

Much has been written about the downside of competition. Many researchers have proposed the notion of cooperation over competition.

Until recently, I wholeheartedly agreed. I wanted my kids to learn to strive for excellence, not the thrill of just winning. I wanted them to learn how to be team players. And while I still want these things for them, I realized that something else was going on here with Jenny Rose. As far as competition was concerned, this was a case of my child being so fundamentally different from me.

A Competitive Spirit

Of a character quality being misidentified as a dangerous flaw.

I've come to see that being competitive is as core a quality of Jenny Rose as cooperation is one of mine. While I will go out of my way to not be one of the pack, she will rush right in there and show her stuff. She wants fast and I want slow. I'm sure we are not the first family members to be polar opposites.

This difference became crystal clear when she asked if she could compete in an ice skating competition. I gave her an immediate *no*, and I wasn't nice about it. "No way," I said. "You are way too young. That's too much pressure."

But Tara Lipinski had made her mark on Jenny Rose. She did not relent. She asked every day. I kept saying *no* but began to consult the experts. Her coach. Other mothers of skaters.

And I watched her on the ice. Having said *no* burst a huge motivational bubble for her. Her interest was waning. Her focus was fuzzy. When I broke down and said that I was considering it, I noticed more changes. Focus. Edge. Drive. Internal motivation.

When my husband and I finally gave her the *yes* after much deliberation, her skating took off. By giving her a concrete goal — the competition — we gave her something to wrap her desire around. Something tangible. And while the pressure would make me nuts, it was her engine.

The message only grew louder when Jenny broke her leg — not on the ice, but on a trampoline — and missed not only a season of figure skating, but the entire soccer season. I was concerned about how we'd keep this energetic kid busy and content for eight weeks while she healed.

Well, I needn't have worried. She was competing in another vein now. She asked her kindergarten teacher for "homework." She begged us to teach her multiplication tables. She wanted to be quizzed constantly from Brain Quest. She went with her dad to her soccer team's games and cheered them on, feeling every loss and win as if they were hers. The kid is competitive from the depths of her soul.

A Competitive Spirit

Jenny Rose has taught me that we are all wired differently. What makes my teeth clench with stress is energizing for her. As long as she plays with good sportswomanship, for her the winning and getting the right answer is a very compelling process. A thrill. I don't have to get it, or even agree necessarily. I guess I just have to praise her, build opportunities for her to succeed and honor the differences between us.

July 1998

"A Competitive Spirit" received an honorable mention in the personal essay category from the Parenting Publications of America in 1998.

Simplicity

If a blueprint existed that could help us simplify our lives, you would think you could find it somewhere in the voluntary simplicity movement, right? Or so I thought when I recently cruised down the mass-market, spiritual non-fiction aisle of my local bookstore.

The idea behind these books, which usually have the word "simple" in the title, is that being less technology-dependent, more material-free can be a richer, more spiritual way to live. This is a captivating notion to those of us who feel as if we are slaves to the jangle of a cell phone, the whimpers and whines of children needing or wanting things, the honk of car horns in a traffic jam, or the jarring ring of a morning alarm clock.

Enthralled by the idea that I might be able to find a way to untangle what feels like an unbelievably complicated life, I bought one of those books. It was written by a Los Angeles couple who left their screenwriting careers to farm the family apple orchard on the East Coast. It was the story of how they traded their fast, shiny cars and superhighway commutes for a slower, less thing-filled life of tractors and acres of land dotted with fruit trees. I was about half-way through the book when I put it down, disappointed. It was written engagingly enough, but it read like a regurgitation of old ideas. It struck me as watered down. Unoriginal.

Then I recalled where I'd heard these ideas before: *Walden.* That classic narrative published in 1854 by Henry David Thoreau in which he voluntarily left his comfortable life in Concord, Massachusetts, and discovered peace and serenity by moving to Walden Pond. I'd never read the book, but the ideas had always compelled me.

Simplicity

So I bought *Walden*, plunged in, and found out something very interesting. It wasn't the easy-to-digest version that my contemporary simple living book was, but this older and dustier tome was far more gratifying. I had to rely heavily on the annotated version, and desperately craved a discussion group, but it was written so that its meaning could be unraveled and thought about in layers. A little like poetry. And uniquely *timeless*.

Thoreau wrote about the joy of a life lived more analytically and closer to the rhythms of nature that rings as true today as it did in the mid-1800s. On techno-dependencies, he wrote: "Our inventions are wont to be pretty toys which distract our attention from serious things." On crowds, he wrote, "Individuals, like nations, must have suitable broad and natural boundaries, even a considerable neutral ground, between them."

I believe *Walden* gave me something to think about precisely because it made me work for it. You've heard the saying *perspiration begets inspiration?*

Experiencing *Walden* motivated me to crack open another old book I had never read but had loads of opinions about: I decided to sit down with the Old Testament — the one that we got as a wedding present and was covered in dust on a high closet shelf.

Turns out, around the same time, just a few miles from my home, a group of women were having a similar experience. They had been studying Jewish history and spirituality with a rabbinical student. After many months of study, they were hungry to go beyond a history that was rife with agenda and point of view. So they begged their teacher to allow them to delve with guidance, chapter by chapter, into the Old Testament. They wanted, like me, to go right to the source to untangle its meaning for themselves.

I was lucky to have found this study group when I combed my area for an adult Bible class. From the very first session, I was again struck by the value of reading from the source. In the first book, Genesis, the men and women are paying an enormous amount of attention to the natural rhythms of life, without the distraction of the bells and whistles of today. They recognize when they benefit from the bounty of the land. They learn from its floods and famines. And they even rest. What's bad about this? In fact, it sounded perilously close to those mass-market, spiritual non-fiction books on simplifying one's life.

Though this experience back to good books would probably make my high school English teacher beam, I've concluded that I probably won't find a blueprint for a simple life in books. Some books will speak to you. Others may leave you cold. It pays to dabble. You may go in lots of bizarre directions — Los Angeles to Concord to Walden Pond to the Holy Land may be a very circuitous route — but sweating through the rich details of a primary source can be its own reward.

August 1998

Enough

Of all the catch phrases that come and go among my family members, there are two words that, when spoken by my children, crawl under my skin, bury themselves, and unravel me. And no, they aren't dirty or slang.

Not enough and its corollary *never enough* are usually followed by *attention, underwear, markers* or *time in the morning.*

And they protest in equal amounts and at similar pitches.

I'm pretty sympathetic when it comes to my daughters' feelings, but this brand of gripe doesn't move me. The way I see it, these kids have plenty and I'm losing patience even though I've tried several different approaches to stop it from going any further. I've empathized. (Works temporarily.) Fought with them. (A bad option.) Or given in. (A really bad option).

I'm ashamed to confess that the approach that works best for me is walking out of the room. I do this so I don't say or do something that I will later regret. It's just that these two little words can get me so enraged. It leaves me with the conclusion that, despite of our best efforts, we have raised ungrateful little children. Then I fantasize about moving to Montana and living on a farm where my kids would get plenty of Mom and Dad, lots of opportunities to wash out their underwear, whittle their own pencils, and more time after milking the cows and gathering the eggs in the morning than they would know what to do with.

Not enough and *never enough* get to me because, let's face it, none of us ever has enough. When my kids moan about this, I want to say, "Me, too — I don't get enough attention, I'm running low on good bras and working pens and not only do I not have enough time in the morning, but all day long."

I'd truly like to give them a better answer than a view of the back of me walking out of the door. But what can I say?

"Yes, kids, you are right, there isn't enough; we'll just have to go our different directions. See you when you are an adult."

"No, kids, there really is enough, it's just that Dad and I are hoarding it for ourselves."

"You think you don't have enough — just take a look at these photos of starving children."

"Enough, what's enough, anyway? I've had enough of your whining."

Just as I was thinking that there was no good solution to this issue, something my husband said got me thinking about another approach. It involved an attitude adjustment, only not on my children's part, but on mine.

My husband said that he believes it is a *good* sign that both of our children complain about not getting enough. Yeah, a *good* sign.

"If only one kid is complaining, then you've got something to worry about," he said. (My husband is an attorney and seasoned negotiator.) "When one person is moaning, it's more likely that some unfair advantage is happening. It's a fundamental justice thing. As long as they are complaining in equal proportions, both are being treated fairly. " (Though he was quick to add that it would be a good sign if neither side was complaining, too, but let's be realistic.)

A parenting approach born out of negotiation strategies. It was a compelling thought — easier for a lawyer to do than for a writer-mother, but worth trying.

So I've taken on a bold new strategy that is still in test mode. I've decided to let my children vent. I'm trying to let them say what they want and not let the words get absorbed into my tired, thin skin. Every time I hear the two little words that set me off, I think, "This complaining is just a reminder of how mentally healthy my children are" or "When I don't respond to their complaints, they should call me Mother Justice."

The point of it all is I'm letting them have their feelings. Allowing them to be heard. But trying to stay cool and remain silent. After all, sometimes it is best to respond by not responding. And that's one of those few advantages I have being a mother rather than a lawyer.

September 1998

How My Mother-in-Law
Saved Halloween

I've hated Halloween for as long as I can remember — ever since a childhood friend decided we should dress up as two parts of a horse one year and I got stuck being the back end.

Adding to my disinclination for this festival of things sweet and scary were news reports that surfaced during the height of my Halloween years about razor blades buried in apples and candy laced with hallucinogenic drugs. Stuff like that really took the treat out of trick-or-treating.

But there was something even more persuasive than my childhood humiliation and potentially harmful attacks on children to keep me from enjoying this orgy for the mouth and parade for the eyes that most kids love. It took me years to see it, but now that I am a parent, I realize that my *own* parents never had a taste for the holiday.

Ours was the barest house on the block, decoration-wise. No orange and black spiders dangled from our door. My costumes were either commercial, flammable and store-bought or some odd assortment drawn from a motley collection of dress-up clothes (except for the one hand-made horse costume that my friend and I constructed). My folks never went door to door with us — they'd arrange it so that we would travel with a group of kids led by some willing parent.

No need to bring out the violins — I've forgiven them. It's just that after my kids were born I concluded that since I wasn't much of a Halloween mom and my husband wasn't much of a fan either, there was a probability that we'd pass this peculiar family heirloom down to our kids. And I wasn't so sure that it was fair to them.

How My Mother-in-Law Saved Halloween

I put the Halloween issue off as long as possible after my first child was born. But when she was three, there was an unexpected intervention.

Who knew that there was a member of our family who was transforming into a pattern-sewing, costume-wearing, house-decorating, more-than-just-candy-providing, trick-or-treating champion of Halloween. By the fall of my daughter's third year, my mother-in-law's transformation was complete. She emerged as a production manager for this annual event, a quintessential hostess of Halloween.

She knew what she was up against and set out to change the face of this holiday. By August, she had screened costume ideas and was on the hunt for patterns at fabric stores.

The costumes were fitted and hand-sewn by the end of September. Over the years these have included such creations as an orange and black clown suit with tall black felt hat studded with orange yarn balls; an over-the-shoulder green felt M & M suit (and a red one for the mother), an exotic belly dancer/fairy princess (custom designed based on my daughter's indecision), a witch with long, black fingernails and 16-inch hat, and Halloween-patterned vests to wear with black bowlers fitted with yellow plastic daisies.

That was Costume Prep. Then there was Choreography. She'd take the day off of work, dress up in her Raggedy Ann costume complete with red yarn wig and striped tights or a wicked witch costume with black nails and green teeth. She'd go to one school with one granddaughter, look critically at costumes on parade, applaud the well-made ones and critique the ill-constructed ones, provide Halloween candy and decorated pencils to the kids and then travel to the other grandchild's school and do it all over again. She gained quite a reputation in educational circles.

Third was the Runway Walk. This meant a trip to a local indoor mall to allow my children to strut their stuff and fill their bags with treats without threat of bad weather.

How My Mother-in-Law Saved Halloween

Lastly was the climax of the day: the Meet and Greet portion of Halloween. My children and their grandmother tricked and treated through the neighborhood while I positioned myself by the door trying to convince myself that providing sweets to the neighborhood children once a year was an okay thing to do. My children were delivered back rather late and completely exhausted, but happy. My mother-in-law, on the other hand, would be beyond energized. Her Halloween high would last for weeks afterwards.

When my parents-in-law announced they were retiring and moving out of town several years ago, I wondered what would become of Halloween. But of all the things to potentially fear on Halloween, this was not one of them. The holiday had imprinted on this family. I don't take a whole day off as she did or hand out candy at school, but I get to the costume parades in the classrooms, have even been known to dress up for the day, and take a whole roll of film to the one-hour processing service at my local drugstore.

I still hate Halloween — I don't care to have all that processed candy in the house, don't like the ramifications of a late night out on school nights and what some of the costumes I see represent about our society. But these feelings are back burner to what my kids get out of it. For them, it is a meaningful event. An entire day devoted to the joys of being a kid. I try to think of it as an ode to Grandma Joyce. Her love of this holiday showed me that with a little desire, persistence and creativity, a loving someone can step in and breathe new life into a family ritual. For saving Halloween in our family, I say, Thanks, Joyce.

October 1998

Gifts: Part One

Over lunches, dinners and coffee over the years, my friend Kate and I have been having this ongoing discussion about how we anguish over giving gifts.

We've decided that we belong to that category of gift givers who take our assignments very seriously. Send us an invitation to an event, ask us to dinner or let the holiday season come upon us and we put selection of the gift high on our to-do list.

Funny thing is, neither one of us think of ourselves as very materialistic. We care more about emotions and feelings than thingamabobs to put on a shelf. But when we have been asked to honor a person, we really care about whether the gift is just right: Does it say *her* all over? Does it fit his taste? Does it meet the occasion? Is it the right price? Does it reflect the nature of the relationship?

Neither one of us has an abundance of time on our hands to shop around for presents, but we work on it until it's right. And that might even mean, in my case, taking something back after wrapping it, because I saw something better later. When it's right, it's oh-so-right. There's nothing like seeing the face of your friend, family member or co-worker as she opens the gift and you know that it was a hit.

But getting there can sometimes feel like more work than the task merits. We review our relationship to that person over the past year, imagine our ultimate goal (that look or gesture), plan our routes, ponder our budgets, call our favorite shops, page through our favorite catalogs, park and repark, call and recall, in search of the right gift. We are fully aware that we are not judged by the size, cost or how long it took us to actually get the gift. But we are our own harshest critics.

Gifts: Part One

Are we nuts? Maybe. We are both painfully aware that focusing on a material symbol may be a reflection of deep, dark insecurities. But that's when I think about some of the gifts I've been given that I cherish.

My favorite gifts are ones with a little piece of the giver in them: Drawings or poems for Mother's Day from my kids. What my husband wrote on a card. Limericks written by my mom and dad. Long-distance birthday phone conversations. That colorized photograph a friend painted. Expressions of love and friendship via fax. A reunion in another town. Rocks picked up during exotic travels. They don't necessarily have to cost anything but time or thought on the part of the giver.

So when Kate and I were yet again having another conversation about how far we go to get the right present, and out of the blue she blurts out," Hey, remember that story *The Gift of the Magi* by O. Henry?"

"Yeah, I think so," I say, struggling to recall the details.

"You know, the one where the wife wants to give her husband a watch fob and can't afford it. So she cuts off all her hair in order to pay for it. At the same time, without her knowing, her husband has purchased a beautiful hair comb for her long, luxurious locks," she says.

"And in the end, they are left with nothing but an A for effort," I add.

"Yeah, that one," she says.

We agreed that this story is a great reminder about intention. That even if the present is a bust (like the time I gave my husband several weeks of lawn service for Father's Day and he later told me it felt like the male equivalent of receiving a frying pan), but the intentions are good, then it counts for something.

This got me thinking about the gifts I've been given that haven't necessarily stood out, the "misses" as opposed to the "hits." I don't think any less of the giver. I can always recall the occasion when the present was given to me and take joy from the fact that he or she spent some time thinking about me.

So why are Kate and I so hard on ourselves with this present-giving business? We don't want to go so far as to chop off our proverbial hair for the right gift, but on the other hand, we don't want to come up with nothing. Kate and I would do better to find some peace on this issue. In the larger, grander scheme of things, Kate, don't you think that if the gifts we give don't work, the time we put in does?

Time to do lunch.

November 1998

Hands

It was with my friend Deb, a body worker and mother who is a stage ahead of me in her parenting journey, that I had my hand revelation.

My hands had been feeling like dead weights, clogged from the wrist to the fingers. Stiff. Achy. It was affecting my work. Early onset arthritis? Carpal tunnel syndrome? Deb didn't think so. She asked me if I was willing to try an experiment.

I'm always game with Deb, so I agreed to sit on her couch with my feet planted on the floor. She asked me to close my eyes and hold out my hands, and then she placed objects, piece by piece, into my hands.

She took something small and fuzzy and put it there — something I later found out was a stuffed animal. She asked me to respond to what I sensed, giving me no further instructions. The stuffed toy struck me as soft, floppy and insignificant. Kind of a ho-hummer.

She placed the next thing in my hands — a rock. "Cold and pointy," I think I said.

Third was a bigger, fluffier stuffed animal. "Better in some ways than the small stuffed thing," I reported, "but kind of limp and dead."

Several other objects came and went: a book, other stones, objects of different textures and weights that inspired distinct emotional reactions. She stopped for a moment, and then she placed something wonderfully soft, warm, firm but fleshy in my hand: it was her own hand. It felt ... perfect.

Such a simple act, holding hands. Flesh against flesh. Fingers grasping fingers. What a warm and confirming act. Joy. Complete satisfaction. "Oh, Deb," I cried out. "Stay right there. It feels so good." We both laughed over the sound of me swooning over a held hand. Deb said my face said it all — one big grin from ear to ear.

That day we talked about the role our hands play in our lives, especially in our parenting. How busy our hands are when our children are little, cradling, diapering, stroking, wiping, feeding, and holding. And how as our children grow, there are fewer and fewer opportunities to touch our children.

We agreed that this was a kind of loss. It is yet another way our children show us they are growing older, forcing us to change a little, too, before we are ready.

We also talked about hands from our children's perspective. How hands are the curious antennae of children. How if we let children explore the world with their hands by digging in the dirt, playing with a model airplane, stroking a cat or holding a trusted adult's hand, we are giving our children a wonderful opportunity. To encourage them to use their natural inquisitiveness to discover the world. How instinctive and beautiful it is for two children to run around touching things — and holding hands.

As for my hands hurting, it was possible, she hypothesized, that they hurt for the chances I may have missed growing up to be allowed to explore. Like a lot of adventurous and creative kids, I got my fair share of "Watch out, you'll get dirty," or "Don't touch that."

A second explanation was that since my children were becoming more independent, I had been losing touch with them, literally. Could hands ache like a mother's heart?

My hands feel better these days since I've become aware of their role in family life. I've since concluded that my hands were calling out to be noticed, as so many bodily aches do. My hands reminded me about the role of touch in my mothering.

The best, of course, is when some kind of touch comes from our children without prompting. My hand adventure taught me to relish these moments because they aren't with us for very long. You know the moments I mean: that occasional bed pounce, surprise hug, wet kiss, or my personal favorite, holding hands.

December 1998

1999-2000

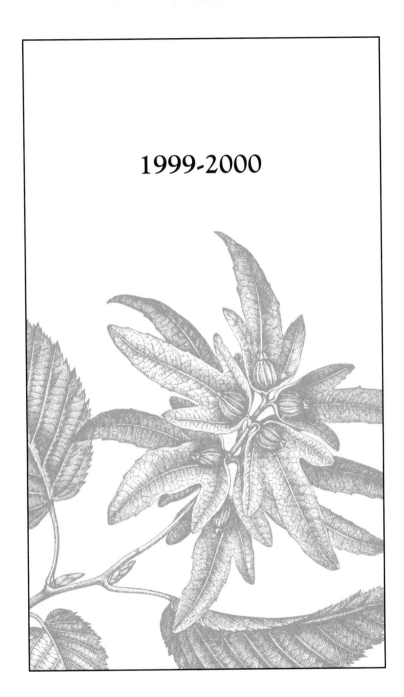

My Journal

I am blessed with thoughtful, supportive and wise friends and family members with whom I share personal, private and psychotic pieces of my life.

But I bear my soul to only one: my journal.

Actually, many journals. They are squeezed into plastic containers and boxes and trunks all over my house. Some are kept high on shelves. Others are under my bed. Each of them is different, depending on my mood, what was available, or my finances at the time. I've got black cardboard sketchbooks, composition books, leather-covered, fabric and water-marked ones. They are lineless and lined, spiral bound and hard backed. I'm not particular, except that they remain private.

That's why I went ballistic when I lost one of my journals. I was headed out of town for the weekend and had placed my journal on my bed, along with my clothes, toiletries and a novel. When I returned from my trip, not having had the time to write, it wasn't in my suitcase. It wasn't in my purse. And it wasn't in my car. Did I take it there meaning to write while I was there and accidentally leave it? Could it have fallen out when I shuffled through my things during my stay? Or worse, did someone pick it up somewhere along the way?

I had been staying at the beach home of my friend's parents. My mind raced with possibilities. Did my friend pick it up? Did her parents? Did someone else? Would they have realized it was mine? I desperately reviewed my current topics. What had I been mulling over recently? What would I have written? What if they read that angry entry about leaving my whole family for the life of a solitary writer? Or letters I'd written giving family members a piece of my mind but didn't send? Or that fantasy I had about that guy from work?

Funny about the timing of things. A few months before this experience I had been thinking of throwing my journals out.

I had three reasons. First, I was thinking that with my children getting older and more curious, it might be time to protect my privacy. Did I want those experiences from the '70s and '80s that I'm not yet ready to share with them so readily available? Second, they were taking up an awful lot of prime space in the house. And third, they were just me, expressing the fleeting feelings of the moment. A lot changes after an entry. Did I want these momentary musings to be left to speak about who I was if I were gone? I deliberated over whether to do it and how, consulting wise women, both journal keepers and not.

My cousin Rachel, a poet, suggested that I review them and highlight the parts that had meaning for me with yellow marker. Or copy the pages so that I could use them for something else. Mary Ellen, a writer with a place of her own and no nosy kids, offered to have me store them at her apartment in a locked box to keep them from intruders. Deb, my friend and body worker, suggested I have a ritual burning of them to honor what they had done for me thus far. I had been seriously considering each of these options when I lost my journal.

In the few days it took me to get through to my friend to get through to her parents to get through to someone at the house, I imagined every worst-case scenario possible. That heart-wrenching scene from *Harriet the Spy* came to mind: Remember when all of her friends find her diary, read about themselves and then reject her?

After a few anxiety-filled days, my friend reported that her parents had not found the book anywhere on the premises.

The book hadn't turned up at home, either. I finally cracked open a new journal and wrote pages and pages mourning the loss of my diary. About how it stung to have my privacy invaded. The idea that

My Journal

I had no control over in whose hands my words were sitting.

Then one August day, three months after my journal had first been missing, I was rearranging the furniture in my bedroom and I moved the bed to vacuum in a tight spot. There, in the dust balls under the bed, lay my spiral bound hardback journal on the floor.

It had never even left the room.

If you believe in life lessons, then you'll be pleased to know that I learned mine that day. I had lost my journal so that I would know how it felt to be without one. Without it, I was miserable.

Now I'm teaching my children about respecting privacy. I took my friend up on her offer to store them for a while. And I started putting some money away to build a wall of new shelving to make room for my journals, so that they will always have a prominent place in my life.

January 1999

A Mother's Ear

Of all the senses we are blessed with when we are born, some grow more sensitive when we become mothers. It's like they become activated.

For one mother, it was her hearing. When her children were newly born, she reveled in the rhythm of their baby breath; she delighted in their squeals; she bathed in the sound of those first words. These were utterly satisfying for her.

But as her children began to use their voices — the voices that she so strongly encouraged — as they told her about their thoughts, their dreams, the details of their day, and as their curious questions came at her like a flock of birds looking to land, the mother's hearing became highly sensitive. She began to hear more than just words. She didn't just empathize, she actually felt their feelings.

She listened well because — more than anything else — this was what she had wanted for herself growing up. She believed it was a way for her to be a good mother.

Her acute listening went on for some years, bringing her great happiness and pride as a mother. The children evolved into the lively, entertaining conversationalists their mother hoped they would be. They were a deep well of thoughts, opinions and stories. She listened joyfully, until one day something strange began to happen to her. When her children spoke to her, she disappeared.

This mother was highly unsettled as she watched her fingers, hands, arms and then torso and legs fade into nothingness. When her children finished speaking, the mother would return to sight.

What was most peculiar about her disappearances was that her children did not notice them. They chatted merrily about their day, not noticing that their mother's body was invisible at the time. They were comfortable because they felt her strong, loving presence in the room with them. They felt this more than anything.

The mother's listening-related disappearances went on like this for a long time, and she gave herself up to her periodic invisibility — until she became ill. She was tense and confused. She no longer experienced joy listening to her beautiful children. The sounds of their voices grated on her and pushed her to the brink. She was unable to hear more than one sound at once. She pushed away most every sound in her life that she used to love, even music. She slept with clenched teeth and a locked jaw.

A friend — another mother — urged her to see a healer. This healer was a woman whose wisdom came in large part from honoring the lessons she learned from her own motherhood.

The healer mother told the weary one that she had been carrying a heavy burden around in her body. The healer mother laid her mother hands upon her and listened to the sounds of her body.

She created a safe and quiet space for the ailing mother. In that quiet room, she sensed her body's voices reawakening. She felt places of warmth. Places of churning. Then she heard a small voice inside saying, "Do you feel me?"

The mother felt a stirring in her chest. "Yes, I do," she said faintly.

"Do you know who I am?" asked the voice.

"I'm not certain," said the woman.

"I am your heart — your crowded heart," the voice said. "I am the space inside that you give away when you listen to your children. I am so full of their stories and their feelings that I am overflowing. You have retained every detail of their lives like a recording and I am unable to carry all of the feelings around anymore. It's very generous of you to listen with your whole being, but you leave yourself with nothing and this is why you become invisible."

The weary mother was stupefied as she listened to the sound of her own heart speaking.

"You can listen and still be visible at the same time. You can give more to those around you when you stay visible," the voice said. "Your children want you reflected back at them, not pieces of themselves."

"How do I do this?"

"Listen to yourself first. Hear your own body's voices. Open up a channel and then become aware of your ears as instruments. Honor them for their ability to listen so well. Dress them up with jewels. Cover them when they are cold. Respect them, don't overuse them. Listen to them like you breathe: take the sounds of your children in, feel whatever it is that you feel, and then let the feelings go. Then you will make room for future details and emotions that your children will share with you."

The mother pondered this advice, and then smiled.

Then the quiet, sacred space in which this conversation was being held folded up and disappeared, leaving the mother face to face with the healer mother who was sitting beside her, smiling.

The formerly weary mother let the conversation with her own heart — facilitated by another mother — filter through her. We all need a safe, quiet space to hear ourselves in, the selves we forget, the selves that sometimes become buried, or invisible, underneath the good intentions we have for our children.

May 1999

Best Friends

Last summer, I had one of those moments that forever changed the way I view myself as a mother.

During intermission at an outdoor rock concert with my pop music-loving preadolescent daughter, as we strolled the grounds where hand-dyed clothes hung in the breeze, jewelry jingled and candles sent incense-aromas into the air, we both reached for the very same tie-dye shirt to try on.

Six presidents, one big war, several smaller wars and a technology boom between us, and my daughter and I were attracted to the same 1960s hippie-inspired tie-dye shirt hanging on a rack at a rock concert?

Whoa. This wasn't just Emily liking what her mom liked. This was me liking what she liked, too. All of this had a kind of eerie effect on me. Was I the mother here or the friend? And what year was it, anyway? I was the giddy peer eager to try on a cool new shirt and I was the same woman who had made certain she was wearing socks underneath her sneakers that night and had packed an extra sweater in her backpack.

Afterwards, I couldn't let that moment go. I looked for clues from my experience with my own mother. I remember thinking that she had good taste, but I wasn't inclined to wear my mother's clothes and we had certainly never grabbed for the same shirt.

Not long after this experience, I was interested to discover that I was not the only mother whose taste gravitated toward the preteen. A flurry of studies were released suggesting that the generation gap between boomer mothers and their daughters had narrowed. We shop at the same stores and listen to the same music. The studies suggested that mothers and daughters are more like friends than relatives.

Two reasons, say researchers, are that the rate of change has slowed since children who grew up the 1960s pushed the limits of social mores; boomer parents had their life-defining experiences in college and graduate school, whereas their own parents' attitudes were shaped by the Depression years or World War II. And, we live in a time of turmoil — safety-wise — that makes teens turn to their mothers to feel more secure.

In one study, teens were asked, "Do you consider any of your family members to be real friends?" Eighty-five percent said yes, and Mom was most often named.

With our T-shirt and these studies in mind, I shouldn't have been surprised when my daughter asked if we could ever be best friends. But it did. I was aware of the loaded nature of the question. So much so that I told her I'd have to think about that for a while.

And when I got clearer on it, I told her that we had something no two best friends could ever have — a relationship by blood, even by spirit, by something very unique called family.

But days later I was distressed over the answer I gave. I had given her a mother answer. She had wanted a best friend answer. Had I reduced our special bond to genetics?

I was on a hunt for a definition of this new mother role. I watched Emily interact with babysitters, fifth-grade friends and young salesgirls. How easily came the flow of conversation on topics like clothes, body image and dating. How simple it was for the salesgirl to say how great Emily looked in that flowery, thin strappy dress without adding any motherly caveats like what she should do about the bra strap.

The advantages for my daughter to view me as her best friend seem clear. If you are best friends with your mom, maybe you don't need to be reminded to bring your glasses case with you or to be asked to write that thank you note. You neutralize the mom part a little bit.

But what about the mother's side? It's tempting to think of our daughters as contemporaries. They are our little women, and we know one another so well, but in the end, we are always carrying their bag, brushing the hair out of their eyes, reminding them to bring an extra sweatshirt. We are always thinking like the parent. We don't get to have the best friend stuff without the backdrop of fussing.

That's when I concluded that the way to be my daughter's best friend is to be her mother first.

August 1999

The House Plant

The day before my daughter turned 11, she got her period.

I don't know how it ranked for her as an experience, but it was a significant marker for her mother. It was my opportunity to put my beliefs to the test — to show her how to admire what her body could do in spite of awkwardness and discomfort. On that day, I kissed her, congratulated her, called my mother and cried. For us all.

The next morning as she trotted off to school, complete with a backpack full of sanitary napkins and a note to the nurse to dispense Advil if needed, I had an overwhelming urge to check the plant.

The plant to which I refer had been living with us since the day my daughter was born. Someone — I can't recall who — brought the basketed green house plant to us at the hospital. For some reason unknown to me or anyone else I've consulted, it has lived heartily for more than a decade, one of the last remaining birth day gifts, a close second to a stuffed dog named Puppy that was bestowed to her that day.

Because this little plant fared so well — as my daughter did — the plant had always been symbolic of my daughter's health and well-being. It thrived no matter where we put it, like she did. It needed water and some attention, of course, but it stayed green and strong even when we forgot (which is not to say that we ever forgot to feed our daughter or give her attention). It's just that our firstborn daughter was an easy-going child, very transportable, adaptable, flexible and healthy — like the plant.

I got into the habit of thinking the plant's health was reflective of my successful nurturing skills — partly because I never was much of a gardener. I played this little mental game with myself — that the plant's health represented my daughter's.

So when I checked it that day — not expecting anything in particular — I noticed that the healthy, thriving green leaves had dwindled to two. Two small leaves flanked the stalk and one of them was starting to turn brown.

I decided to move it to another location in the house — a trick that had worked before. A day or two later, no change. Two scrawny leaves.

I added dirt. Miracle-Gro. Nothing.

Meanwhile, my daughter was doing quite well with her new status in life. She had a renewed, quiet confidence. Not long afterwards, when the good weather came, she wanted to go places by herself: bike around the neighborhood, meet friends at the ice cream store.

I also noticed that my outside plants were all doing well. That's when the idea hit: Put the plant outside.

After two days in the sun on my back deck among the flowers, a new growth sprouted. A tiny little green, perky leaf began to grow from what was an almost dying vine.

Okay, I thought. This plant clearly needed to be outside of my controlled environment to thrive. After all, how could I compete with the elements of nature?

This connection still existed between this plant's well-being and my daughter's. By reaching this rite of passage, my daughter had crossed to a place outside of my control. She was going to menstruate on her own schedule. She was going to be having experiences that I wouldn't be around to oversee. To really thrive, she'd be needing the sunshine, the rain, fresh air and being with other growing things.

A few days after I first noticed the new growth, I was washing dishes and looking out our kitchen window at my botanical/ parenting accomplishment and what did I see but a fat gray rabbit chewing on the plant.

I ran like a crazed woman out my back door to shoo the critter away. And that's when I realized that even though my daughter had become an integral part of the cycle of nature, she was going to be exposed to nature's ways, and I wouldn't always be able to protect her.

Sure enough, that varmint got every available piece of green off of that house plant. I hung onto the plant — or really the basket — for months afterwards, even after a green algae sheen covered it. When it was clear that nothing was going to sprout out of it anymore, I realized it was time to let it go.

So on the day when my daughter went to her first boy-girl party, I buried what was left in the soil in our backyard compost heap and laid the basket to rest.

October 1999

The Biology of Marriage

Early in my marriage, when I'd see older couples sitting together at a restaurant table, not speaking, I'd elbow my husband and whisper with a critical tone in my voice, "Honey, I hope we'll never be like that — I hope we always have something to talk about." He'd nod, letting me stew in my own judgment over this type of marital behavior.

I had opinions about other couples not talking at restaurants because it seemed to me that if you weren't talking to your mate, you were headed for trouble. Perhaps I put too much stock in words because I rely on them professionally, but I believed that good relationships meant lots and lots of non-stop, late-into-the-night discussions about this and lots of that.

Of course, this was easy to believe before I became a mother. Before I became intimate with the parent version of exhaustion, the asleep-before-you-hit-the-pillow form.

But now, 15 years into marriage, I can say without a doubt that while communication is still a huge factor on my list of attributes for a good, sound relationship, I've been learning that this isn't all there is.

And I'm not talking about sex, either *(not that there's anything wrong with it!)*

I'm talking about the time toll on a long-term relationship.

I have a friend, married many years longer than me, who told me once that she thought marriage was a like a double helix DNA strand that we all learned about in high school biology class. You know that twisted-figure-eight-upon-figure-eight that's considered one of the building blocks of life?

The Biology of Marriage

I wasn't paying much attention in high school biology class, so I went looking for information about this scientific symbol. The metaphor is interesting. DNA is made up of sugars and phosphates that form a molecule. Even I recall that molecules are the basic form of life. Hmm, a long-term relationship as a basic form of life? The strands are linked by hydrogen bonds called base pair linkages. Could these be the moments of connection we feel with our mates?

By design, the strands of the double helix intersect and bow out. I like to think that the intersecting lines coordinate with the dating period, for example. That time when you and your partner were on more of the same page. It didn't matter where you went, just that you were together, remember?

But then, after children, you move in another, necessary direction. Into domestic or professional or just plain no-time-to-go-with-the-flow stuff. The lines bow out, reflecting a time where you are still united as a unit and can connect periodically — but just out there doing what you need to be doing.

But then, something breaks open. Your children become a little more independent; or you have one great night together that reminded you of why you got together in the first place; or you just plain begin to miss what you used to have and you think about trying to resurrect it again. And then, hopefully, you move slowly back towards one another again. In small baby steps.

My friend's point was this: Healthy marriages go in and out of "in syncness". They would be dysfunctional if they didn't. The strands of the double helix must bow out and in steadily for the structure to stay afloat. If the two lines ran parallel to one another, the whole structure would collapse. There's something organic in this — something chemical that drew you to one another in the first place, a connection already forged.

It may be a struggle to keep this biological big picture idea of a marriage in view. But there are moments that remind me of its truth. Some time ago, after my husband had put the kids to bed and the dinner dishes were done, he was sprawled out on the couch with the TV remote in his hand watching Comedy Central (or was it a ballgame?). I just collapsed on the edge of the couch next to him, too tired to put another load of laundry in, make any more calls, clean any more surfaces or pay any more bills. He turned off the TV and we just sat there in the dark sharing a moment of silence. Neither of us wanted to do or say anything in particular. We just rested there together, contentedly, like those older couples I see in the restaurants, sitting there together, peaceful, silent. It felt like a reconnecting though we weren't saying a word. Refueling without doing a thing. For a long time. It was really magical. And I thought, who else in the world could I do this with? Who else would I want to do this with? And then, wordlessly, we went to bed.

November 1999

A Mother's Mission Statement

I will try to remember that children come into this world absolutely, positively perfect.

I will acknowledge that nature accounts for only half of what children will become — the other part is nurture.

I will keep in mind that it takes no effort to love my children, only to show them that I do.

I will say yes to my children whenever possible.

I will say no to my children if what they are asking is more than I can give at the time, and I will be okay about this.

I will provide my children with lessons, trips, parties and trinkets, but I will never promise any of these.

I will attend my children's plays, shows, competitions, graduations and other important events, but I will not beat myself up if, for some reason out of my control, I can't make it.

I will teach my children how to keep themselves clean, well-fed, and healthy but I will not hover over them to ensure all of these things.

My own health and well-being comes first, because if I'm not doing well, everyone else isn't.

My marriage is up there with health and well-being, because most everything else in my family springs from this well.

I am allowed to talk on the phone with friends, exercise, take a class, go out to lunch, buy a new dress or take a weekend for myself without feeling like I'm neglecting someone.

A Mother's Mission Statement

When my children show or tell me that they are feeling neglected, I will not dismiss their feelings. I will make an effort to find out what's really going on without feeling guilty.

I will not try to be best friends with my children, because they are my children first and they have friends of their own, as do I.

I am a working mother, and so, like working fathers I can have help around the house, which includes housekeeping, dry cleaning and the occasional take-out dinner.

Each of my family members is entitled to privacy — but parents more so.

I will encourage my children, support them, praise them, but honor their differences.

I will be very careful about my word choices and my tone of voice when I speak to my children.

I will ask that my children be more careful about theirs.

My children are on loan to me for a short while, shorter than they will live in the world independently (hopefully).

My children are my responsibility, but I am not their boss. A mother is a spiritual leader to her children.

I will understand that I am growing, too, alongside my children.

I will accept the fact that I can impart knowledge to my children, not necessarily wisdom.

And I will be aware that I can teach wisdom only by being wise.

December 1999

Money in Sight

I am one-half of a two-income family and, according to everything I have heard and read, we are supposed to be the living example of the financial arrangement best suited to paying bills and other living expenses.

Why is it, then, that when we manage to cover all of our bills for the month, it is a pleasant surprise?

Recently, I found myself wondering if it's just me. Was it possible to manage our money so that covering our expenses each month would no longer be a surprise? And if I couldn't immediately change what was coming in, how about what was going out?

So I brushed up on money management by reading a few best-selling books on the subject and put us on a budget and tried a few tricks: I organized my paper ones, fives, tens and twenties. I paid cash for everything one week just to see if that made a difference. (It didn't.) When my psychedelic-sixties-inspired printed checks ran out, I ordered gray government-document looking ones so that the money in my checkbook would look more like actual dollars. I took all the coins in the house to the bank to turn them from silver and copper into a more manageable paper version. I opened up a home equity loan account to help reduce our credit card expenses at a lower percentage rate. I cut down on extras like take-out dinners, checkout line purchases, and high-priced haircuts. I even hired a financial consultant.

These changes made me feel better — like I was being proactive — but at month's end there was no discernible difference. Paying off every bill was still a tight squeeze.

Right around that time, I was searching for a birthday card for a friend and came upon an attractive one by the artist and writer Sark with the headline that read "How to Relax About Money."

I took this as a sign.

The card said:

"Make friends with money. Money is like love; the more you give away, the more comes back. When any money flows in for you, it's time to help others. Money was invented to be shared."

That's when I decided on a new tactic. My approaches weren't working. I needed to change the way I thought about money.

Money is, after all, a little bit like fluid. It's a shared and valued commodity flowing as easily as water from a faucet. So, I bought the card, pinned it up on my office bulletin board and read it often, hoping its insights would change the flow of our money.

I began to experiment. I marked a folder with the words "Possible Donations" on it and set aside solicitations for various causes and projects. But when they came due, I'd hold back asking myself how we could justify this expense when we had credit card debt to pay?

Then one day I over-tipped a waitress, on purpose. A few days later, I handed the last of the change in my purse to three Boy Scouts selling a type of popcorn my family will not eat. I gave my daughter more money than she really earned for cleaning out a linen closet and I wrote a check to the synagogue over and above our dues.

I realized that I had been gripping our money too tightly. Soon some interesting things happened.

My domestic landscape showed up as just a bit more bountiful. I saw more than enough seating, a stocked pantry and plenty of clean sheets. Instead of making lists of things to acquire, or needing fixing or updating, I found myself focusing on how lucky we were to have working appliances and walls without holes. Instead of seeing our home as filled with hand-me-down furniture, I focused on appreciating its family history and its cushy, if somewhat tired, comfort.

Soon, the universe seemed to pop with other abundances. I earned an unexpected $100 when a publisher asked to reprint an article I had written and days later received an invitation to a retreat that I really wanted to attend. Guess what it cost to go? My husband and I received an unexpected check from the government because we had overpaid our taxes. And then, just when the steering wheel and brakes went our on our mini-van, a 50 percent discount coupon arrived in the mail from our auto mechanic.

Though our money is stretched to the limit and once in a while a check may bounce, I'm trying to think of it less like rubber and more like liquid. Rubber snaps and breaks clean. Sure, liquid is messier, but when it splatters, it leaves drops behind.

January 2000

Perimenopause

Last summer, my body gave me a foreshadowing of things to come.

In May, I got my period as I have every month since I was 11, with some breaks for pregnancies and breastfeeding. But in June, no period. I made a mad dash to the pharmacy to rule out the obvious — and, thankfully, not pregnant. I scheduled an appointment with my nurse midwife to rule out illness. A clean bill of health. But in July, it was a no show. And by August, still nothing.

That summer, my period stopped for three months running. And then, as mysteriously as it left, it showed up again in September like nothing odd had ever happened.

I share these intimate details with you not to provide you with more than you'd ever like to know about my hormonal cycles, but to make a point.

Like millions of other women, my period has been a huge part of my life. Huge in the sense that every month contained a full range of premenstrual symptoms. Huge in the hours logged for cramp pain. For most of my reproductive life, I've been impacted, mostly negatively, by my monthly cycle.

And then my period just stopped coming. With pregnancy and illness ruled out, you would think it would have been cause for celebration. Finally, a break from all that discomfort. But no. The truth was, I was completely thrown.

For almost 30 years, I had defined myself as a woman with premenstrual syndrome. I viewed my life through the eyes of a woman whose body would fill with fluid, pushing the scale up several pounds for a few weeks and then down for a few. I was a woman whose body sent me hunting for intensely salty and sugary foods and then couldn't thwart me from eating them in large amounts. I was a woman whose body stew churned up anxiety that would get so big that I'd imagine horrible things happening to me or my family and worry needlessly about things I had no control over.

The calendar has been a dictator of my moods, aches and tone of voice. I could justify each because, after all, they were the result of something bigger than myself, something systemic that makes women women. I have never used the fallout around my period as an excuse — at least publicly — but I have always had it in my back pocket. That the chips and chocolate bars were a temporary desire because I was two days from getting my flow. Or that my protruding belly was water build-up — not fat — because I was eating salt and sugar before my period. That the impatient tone I used with my husband and children was linked to fluctuations of body chemicals that would soon subside.

And so, last summer, with no emotional or physical events building toward a crescendo, I temporarily lost my sense of who I was. I had defined myself all these years as a woman with PMS. It explained me to myself and, when necessary, to others. But here I was, no longer premenstrual and having sensations that I couldn't ascribe to something else. If they weren't about being PMS-y, as we all came to call it in my family, oh, no, What did that mean they were?

During that three-month stretch with no period, my gurus included a nurse midwife, gynecologist, homeopath and nutritionist. They informed me that I was experiencing something very normal — though a tad early at age 40 — and that there was no way to know how long it would stay away, but it would most likely return before leaving forever.

They urged me to try and relax and not worry about when it would return. That I was in perimenopause, with the emphasis on the *peri*, which means "near, enclosing or surrounding". This is the part women so often forget about — that menopause doesn't just happen one day. We move toward it, in fits and starts, sometimes ungracefully, over a period of up to 15 years.

I was grateful for these assurances and, in the end, for this experience. Because it was yet another reminder, in a life full of them, that we think we have control when we really don't. It gave me the chance to think of myself outside the realm of a cycle. Soon there will be no countable days acting as a reference point for my sensations or behavior. A little scary, yes, but now that I know it's imminent, I'm thinking I can appreciate the predictability of the discomfort of my periodic cycles — and take some time to prepare for the final goodbye.

March 2000

Groups

Between the time I served the pepperoni pizza and the strawberry whipped cream cake to nine 12-year-old girls at my daughter's birthday slumber party, I was reminded of why I've spent most of life staying away from groups.

Don't get me wrong: My daughter tells me that the party was a success. Even I had a good time — though I'm still recovering. Watching these girls relate to one another, running the gamut from serious to silly, insinuating to sensitive, took me back to my own experience in groups — or rather to my insistence on steering clear of them. Before I had children, I stayed far from group activities because I found them to be, how shall I say it — *challenging.*

Growing up, I preferred solitary pursuits: reading, writing, walking, making and listening to music. I wasn't the one running for class president. I dropped out of the Girl Scouts after just a few meetings and wasn't much of a team sports player in high school. I didn't like to compete much on any front — I wasn't even apt to vie for the attention of a high school heartthrob if I sensed someone else was vying, too. I like a party every now and then, but I go for the smaller dinner party gatherings. I'm not big on crowds — ever since I was lifted off the ground by masses of people headed toward the gates at a rock concert years ago.

But since becoming a parent, I have found myself in groups — a lot. There I was, hosting an all-night party with continuous meals for nine children in a home I rarely use for entertaining grownups. That night, I realized that I've become a part of a vast array of groups. I am part of a group of parents who throw slumber parties. But I'm also among a group of parents who gather regularly at the rink as their children skate and compete. I help organize the holiday events at school in my role as room parent, along with several other room parents. I'm one of many parents who pick up and drop off their middle school children at school dances. I'm a part of a group of parents whose children act in a local theater troupe. I'm a member of a group of parents whose children play soccer, whose children attend camp and go to birthday parties. I'm also a part of a larger group of mothers who work outside of the home as well as inside and women who have been pregnant.

What struck me the night of my daughter's party was that, despite my natural tendencies, I had, over the years, without noticing it, become a group person. Somehow, I had even learned to thrive in them.

Having children can do that to a person. You want to make that room parent experience a good one, for your own sake as well as your child's.

If I think back to that very first parenting-related foray into a group of strangers it would have to be that first Lamaze class. My husband and I sat on the floor with six other couples who, like us, were about to embark on a life-altering experience. We weren't coming together as people interested in the same things. It wasn't a book club, swim team, support group or work-related event. We probably wouldn't have chosen these folks as friends. But we gathered weekly in an overly air conditioned community center room together, a little bit fearful and a little cocky. And we met a woman there, a writer who had just had a baby and was looking for women to interview for a book. Sensitive to writer mothers, I gave her my number. It later turned into a friendship, professional networking partnership, and playdates for my kids — an experience in a group that was *positive*.

Groups do that for us. They can be energizing. Stimulating. Productive. Fun. They can surprise us with outcomes. They are a natural byproduct of parenthood.

They can also be challenging. Draining. Tiring. Frustrating. Loud. Even unproductive.

It's a gamble. A gamble that, over time, pays off more than I first thought, even if it takes a few days to bounce back.

May 2000

God

It was 1965. I was in Mrs. Rosensweig's first grade class at Charles W. Henry School in Philadelphia. I was six and a half.

Mrs. Rosensweig was standing at the blackboard with her pointer when out of the blue, the classmate seated next to me whispered in my ear, "Ellen, do you believe in God?"

It was a question that could throw a girl, but as it happened, around that time I had been asking my parents about God. We were not a religious family, nor did we hang out in organized religious circles. Ours was a mostly secular life punctuated with some Jewish holiday observances (Passover) and some non-Jewish ones (we had a Christmas tree each year as well as Easter egg hunts.) Any sense of God was most likely to come from my parents. But when it didn't, I was moved to ask them, "Do we believe in God?"

My dad told me to ask my mom. My mom said that she just wasn't sure.

And so, having done the research, I felt justified in responding to this classmate on this particular day by answering truthfully, "Do I believe in God? Well, I'm not sure, but I don't think so." She took my answer and turned it into a game of Telephone, whispering to the little girl next to her, "Ellen doesn't believe in God, pass it on."

All the excitement brought Mrs. Rosensweig to my desk. She demanded to know what was being said and would I share it with the rest of the class. And that's when the little interviewer beside me blurted out, "It's Ellen, Mrs. Rosensweig. She says she doesn't believe in God."

God

Remember, this was the early 1960s. Mrs. Rosensweig had a number of choices that day and unfortunately for me, she leaned in closer, and using her pointer for emphasis, said in front of the entire class, "Ellen, if you don't believe in God, how then do you explain how you got here this morning? How do you explain how the trains and cars go? How do you explain how the universe was created?"

I'll never forget the sensation of every first grader's eyes boring through me as Mrs. Rosensweig made an example of me that day, railing on and on, making my confusion about God only more so and not allowing me the chance to speak or have my questions answered. She gave me the impression, at a very impressionable age, that if you were honest about how you felt about God or were questioning the existence of God at all, you would probably get a public tongue lashing.

I believe that on that very day, I laid my muddled feelings about God to rest. It wasn't worth it, I thought.

Twenty-five years later, it was my children's questions about God, the afterlife and the soul that rustled up these buried memories of a young girl who never got her questions answered. I knew one thing — my children were going to have their questions explored.

And explore we did. When my children were the age to begin religious school, we joined a synagogue, tentatively, with the idea that we'd try it for a year and then see.

After a few months as a member, I felt a tug to venture into the building and consider some adult education classes for myself.

From the very first session, a whole new terrain made itself known to me. I began to see the rich history present in the holidays, the rituals and the texts. But in a class on God led by the rabbi, two healing moments took place. I discovered that I was not the only one who had ever questioned God's existence.

Others in the class had, too. I was reminded that philosophers and writers had for centuries pondered the nature of God. Not just me. I also learned that history is full of people who argued with God and no one was ever struck down dead from their questions.

God

They certainly weren't lectured at by a teacher with a pointer. They were enriched by these disagreements.

After this, I was hungry to learn more. And so began a rich spiritual journey that I like to think motherhood set me on. Or was it Mrs. Rosensweig?

March 2000

"God" earned a Crystal Award from the Association for Women in Communications in 2000.

What I've Learned from People Without Children

A confession:

On particularly long days when I've been asked to counsel, support, guide, advise, discipline or cajole my children, I've comforted myself by comparing my life as a parent with the lives of people I know who are not. I've soothed my cranky and overstimulated head by concluding that while people without children appear to have more freedom, I'm gaining all of this wisdom about the human condition because, after all, I am raising children.

I don't mean to add to the already heated discussions that crop up over inequities between parents and non-parents over promotions in the workplace or noise levels in restaurants. But I will admit that I have often turned to fellow parents and have whispered with some self-importance that our friends who aren't parents couldn't have a clue about what it's like with children.

To everyone I've ever said it about, please forgive me. We parents sometimes say these things to ourselves because we're tired and, frankly, envious. Because though we love our children, we also loved the parts of our lives we had before we had children — and you who do not have children in your life get to live it. Every day.

But as my children have inched closer to preadolescence, I am no longer able to puff myself up with this thinking. Recently, I've collected incredible pearls of wisdom from people I know without children. Insight on what might be going on in my children's emotional life. Perspective on what's going on in their day. And even some common sense about how to take care of myself, which in turn allows me to be a better parent.

What I've Learned from People Without Children

Let me explain.

I first noticed this phenomenon a few years ago as I sat talking with friends who don't have kids in a gloriously quiet, childless apartment. We were talking about my preadolescent daughter, who was growing more sensitive about her body, and it got us talking about our own memories of that time. How our mothers responded to our changing bodies — or how they didn't respond.

I was struck at how these women recalled their memories from the perspective of being a daughter and without the confusion of also being a mother. Being a mother put me too close, too worried and too entwined. My perspective about my changing body when I was younger was all mixed up with my feelings and fears for my children. But for these women without children, it was as if it were yesterday.

At that moment I realized that people without children have got something parents don't have. They aren't sitting as close as we are. They've got perspective — the big picture with an uncomplicated angle on being the offspring.

I began to listen and watch for more of it. Smart helpful advice sprang forth from all sorts of people in my life who don't have children. Friends. Acquaintances. Aunts and uncles. Skating coaches. Dance teachers. Really young teachers at school.

It happened in a conversation I had with a male friend who lives alone. We were talking about middle school. While I was focused on the parental side of it all — the new location and academic challenges — my friend reminded me of how difficult it might be for my daughter emotionally. How critical other kids could be, the new pressures of more homework, the tension between trying to fit in while you simultaneously try to become an individual. His memories were much closer to my daughter's reality than mine — they were a wake-up call to me to switch my focus to her feelings. I had forgotten about how it could be because I was mired in being the mother.

And then, there was what I learned from these childless people by sheer observation.

What I've Learned from People Without Children

Ever notice how well put together people who don't have children in their home appear? True — you could argue that they simply have more time to fuss over themselves. But watching them do it and benefit from it is a model for how to take care of oneself. I've noticed that when I take better care of myself, it always seems to lead to taking better care of my children.

I'm not talking about anything complicated — just about the simple, good-for-you things that we all used to do before having children. Like seeking moments of solitude. Honoring our needs without guilt. If we parents do these things, we tend to feel that it is at our children's expense.

We don't grow up in our children's generation. That's already one huge culture gap between us and them. But I'm thinking that people without children — the thoughtful ones — can help parents bridge that gap. I'm grateful for what I've picked up from these people, but in the end, it's the children who will benefit most.

June 2000

Night Light

My brave little eight-year-old — the tough ice skating competitor, fierce soccer player, risk taker who climbs to the top of our minivan and barrels herself down extremely high pool slides — is afraid of the dark.

For as long as I can remember, she has insisted on sleeping with a light — turned on — in her view.

One evening, probably after writing a check for the electric bill, I decided that it was time for her to face her fears and sleep in the dark like the rest of us.

So I had a chat with her and put forth the argument that she was getting older and that it was a waste of energy to leave lights on during the night. I appealed to her sense of responsibility. To my delight, she agreed to try it for a night. And it worked for one and a half.

We've tried all kinds of combinations: leaving the bathroom light on, installing a night light in her room, keeping a lamp lit or the overhead light on, and then turning them off later in the evening. Nothing worked consistently. I was stumped — I kept telling myself that this was one tough little kid who wasn't afraid of anything — but we couldn't lick this electric issue.

Then one evening, a light bulb went off in my head.

"Angel Cookie," I asked, using one of my many pet names for her and mustering all the energy I could for this rare, calm, before-bed conversation, "Do you think you could tell me why you are afraid when we turn the lights off? Are you afraid of something in the closet?"

"No," Angel Cookie said, confidently.

"Well, what about under the bed?" In my mind I was fast-forwarding through every scary book I'd ever read.

"Nope," she replied, equally sure.

"What about a memory of something you saw — on TV perhaps?" I was sure this was going to be it — validating my decision to keep her from watching scary shows.

"No, no, no," she said, getting irritated.

"Well, do you know what it is then?"

"Yes," Angel Cookie said, "It's because in the dark, I can't see myself."

Couldn't see herself. I was dumbstruck. I saw it from her perspective: Very little would frighten me more than not being able to see myself, dark or no dark. I gave her a hug and a kiss and offered her no words that night — because for the first time I couldn't find any.

Later I thought about how children are so much closer to their feelings than we are — we who are distracted by work, children and electric bills. While I'm not crazy about having the electric company benefit from my daughter's sense of safety, I'm giving up on the night light thing. It's a few extra greenbacks I don't mind spending and that night, Angel Cookie made me understand some things that I clearly had not before. We aren't always ready to conquer our fears because someone else — even if it's someone who loves us — tells us we should be ready. And she made me think about why we are so in need of light: because in it we can see ourselves, and if we can see ourselves, then perhaps we feel that other people can see us, too. And that night, I saw my daughter — and her fears — at close range.

July 2000

Going Away

Your days become interrupted with dreams of getting away. It has been more than a decade since you last traveled somewhere with your life partner that wasn't about visiting family or friends. You are thinking about how you might get off the roller coaster that is your life. Away from carpools, bill paying, meal making, phones ringing and the paper pushing.

Friends of yours — people whose lives are a lot like yours, with children and work — take the plunge and go. Far. Across the ocean. You happily agree to care for their children for the last leg of their trip. This works out well because you get to see that just-got-off-the-plane look on their faces.

That look. So rested and adventured. Lips turned up into smiles that don't fade after the first "hello." You don't need to hear details. You just want the brochure and the telephone number.

It isn't the most responsible thing you ever did — there's college to save for and an upcoming bat mitzvah. But you cross your fingers and ask your in-laws to babysit. They say yes. You thank whatever form of higher spirit you tend to thank in cases like this.

Then you start saving. And reading. You read up on the country. Your friends lend you language tapes. You actually study these. You read maps. Your trip across the ocean becomes what you think about in addition to thinking about your work, your children and the items you need to get on your weekly visit to the grocery store.

Your leaving date quickly approaches and you take on what you think is the hardest part: putting life with your children down on paper so that your in-laws will know what to do. You type in the wake-up times and bus schedule and the after-school classes and lessons. You leave numbers for reliable neighbors and every person you think of as a friend. It makes you take stock of who you can count on in your life. You think about that one for a while.

You alert the school. You wrap everything up that you can at work and at home, including things like when the recycling goes out and where to put the mail. You even update your will.

You think, this is exhausting. *I hope the trip is worth all of this.*

(Note to self: Don't forget to leave the pediatrician's and dentist's number and your homeowner's insurance policy carrier and the address of the nearest video rental store.)

No wonder you are stressed out and need a break. Look how much you do.

You thought this was hard. You were wrong. The hardest part comes four days before you are supposed to get on that plane. Your father-in-law becomes sick. He is admitted to the hospital. Uh oh. You fret and you worry and you support your in-laws as best you can. There's no way you could go now. But everyone, including your in-laws, tells you it will be okay. He's going to be fine. But you aren't sure. Your friends with the faces that prompted you to go tell you about all the things that almost kept them from going. You feel a little better.

And then you go.

You land and the details of the life you lead quickly settle in the back seat. You inhale new smells. Your ears take in different sounding car horns. You lay your eyes on train stations that look like museums and you eat candy with packaging logos you don't recognize and buildings are colors that you don't ever see in your part of town. You begin to speak and think in full and complete sentences that also include adjectives you haven't used in a long while.

You don't read anything for 10 days that isn't a road sign or a map or a menu. You especially like the menus because you think to yourself, someone is cooking *just for me.* You start to listen to your body again and it says, *I'm hungry.* Or, *I'd like to sit down now.* Or, *I want to go there.*

Going Away

So you let it do what it wants because you have no other choice. All of the parts of you are very content. Even though you think about your children — a lot — and you talk about them even more, you are aware deep in your soul that you are feeding it. You are replenishing and refilling your well. Making more to give when you get back. That's why you needed to go.

When you get back, well, you thought making the schedule and leaving your father-in-law were difficult. Difficult was yet to come. Your children jump on you with delight. You all get along great for about eight hours. Then, you get the business. You take it because you know you must. You resist for a while, but the details move back into the front seat. You can't find your garage door opener. *Look at that pile of mail. Here, Mom, you gotta fill out this form. Ring. Crackle. Crackle. Eeeeeeeerrrrrrrr. Connect. You've got mail: 80 messages.* Was it all a dream?

But then you tell some friends about your trip. They look at your face. They even listen to your details. One of them says he is seriously considering doing it next year. You encourage him and provide him with the particulars, because this is clearly a gift that is meant to be passed along, even if it is short lived.

August 2000

A Perfect Place

We all need a place that isn't fully loaded or charged with emotion. For grownups, these places are hard to find. I could tell you where they *aren't*.

But for kids, I have noticed, the car is a perfect place.

When I'm driving with my daughters, while I am partly focusing on the traffic and partly lost in personal thought, they are in a wholly perfect place. They are free of responsibility and expectation (other than to sit buckled and not attack a sibling). They are like great winged creatures, eyes alert to the world passing by from a (slightly) aerial view. (We have a van.) They can think about anything that strikes their fancy, muse on it and say it aloud, too.

And say it they do. The car ends up being the place where great issues are discussed. It was the place where we analyzed the behavior of a fair-weather friend. Where room arrangement ideas first sprung. Where I first heard about skating and dramatics accomplishments and academic disappointments. Where we first started talking about God.

If the radio happens to be on, political questions are raised. "What's nuclear disarmament, Mom?" Or after a long (delightful) silence, an admission of guilt: "Wanna know something I did?" There might be something visually striking on the road, and then it's "I've got an idea for my room!" Or maybe there's just the time and space to consider some plan yet to be hatched. "Mom, I'm gonna DO it, I'm going to clear out my whole closet and rearrange my desk!"

That the car is a place of questions, confessions, ideas and motivation makes sense to me. The car is the epitome of a perfect place for a kid. I can think of three reasons right off the bat: It is an enforced place of rest while you get to move at the same time. Mom or Dad are a captive audience. And it is a neutral zone.

There's no ownership in a car. It's like space. There's little to fight over other than a bit of extra seat or perhaps some more legroom. There are no doors to slam (when they are belted) and no personal items to accidentally borrow and no television clickers to grab.

But a car is still a noisy, stimulating place. There's the sound of the wind against the body, the *rrrrr* of the engine, the radio and street noises. Yet kids are able to get neutral. Get inside themselves. Despite potential distractions.

Watching my children in the car got me thinking about places where I've experienced this feeling. Trains came to mind. Airplanes, too, when there wasn't turbulence. But unless you are in the habit of leaving your children often for business or other travel, it is a few-and-far-between thing to find an actual place where you can go and "get neutral" on a fairly regular basis.

Imagine a place where there is little to get you hot and bothered. A place where we could quiet things down enough to ask questions about our lives. Allow a deep feeling to surface. Clear out our minds enough to catch a great idea. Get motivated to do something we've been wanting to do.

A friend of mine, a busy mother with three children, told me about an experience she had recently that gave me hope of finding such a place that didn't involve getting on a train or going far, far away from my children.

She was with friends who were mothers at one mother's new house. There must have been at least five or six small children. They gathered to celebrate this new home and they wanted to ritualize it. Babysitterless and with time constraints, they decided to take just a few moments to form a circle. They came together in the woman's kitchen (a place usually reserved for chaos) and, arm in arm, chanted a little, sang a little, swayed a little, honoring the moment. Yes, it was noisy. Yes, it was distracting. But as soon as the kids saw their mothers huddled together like this, they settled down, some watching, some leaving them be. But they must have sensed that something bigger than their desire for a snack was taking place. They allowed their mothers the chance to mark the moment.

Another lesson from the children. If they can go to a place inside, by themselves, despite goings-on around them, so can we. For our kids, it's the car. (Maybe for us, too, when traffic isn't heavy.) But we can take back this childhood ability to claim a moment, no matter what else is going on around us. It's easy to use our children as a reason never to take it, but when we do, we've done more than a little something for ourselves and perhaps a whole lot for our children.

September 2000

Gifts: Part Two

Some time ago, I wrote about how my friend Kate and I angst over giving the right gift. How we came to the conclusion that, like the story of the husband and the wife who exchange gifts that are unusable in Gift of the Magi by O. Henry, that the giving is the thing. Two years later, I've had a chance to rethink that conclusion.

After weeks of being stuck on what to give my husband for a birthday gift last year, I had a moment of clarity and came up with what I thought was a present to end all presents.

I wanted to give him something relaxing, soothing and truly escapist. Something that really said, *splurge — it's your birthday!* So I settled on an afternoon at a day spa.

Everyone I know of who has had the luxury of this experience will attest that it is something special. What could possibly be wrong with it?

Well, there was indeed something wrong with it, and I should have seen the signs from the start.

When my husband tore open the envelope that informed him of his afternoon of pampering, I was smiling ear to ear, waiting for his bursts of joy. What I saw instead was a quizzical, not-so-sure-about-this look.

"Hmmmmm ..." he said, which I know now is not the response you want to a gift. When I pressed him, he said he was "open to the experience," but he clearly had his reservations. "It wasn't quite what I had expected," he explained.

A second indicator came the afternoon of his scheduled, virgin spa experience. I was milling around the shopping center with extra time before picking him up and ran into a male friend of ours, who, when I told him where my husband was, snorted with laughter, saying, "*Really? Really? A spa?*" When he walked off, I swear he was still laughing.

Then the third bad sign: When I picked my husband up, I thought that I would have to scoop him off the floor. Instead, he walked out, feet firmly planted, his face redder and cleaner than before. He offered up a half smile, nothing compared to the one I've seen after a long bike ride or two sets of tennis.

I asked him what he thought about the pedicure.

"It was okay," he replied unenthusiastically.

"And the manicure?"

"Fine."

"Okay — what about the facial?"

"Weird."

"Weird?"

"Yeah, weird."

"And the massage?"

"That was good," he offered. He liked the massage.

Later, after my shock wore off, and I was scheming ahead to next year, we talked about presents we had known and loved — and not loved. He compared the present I gave him with another dud — the time I gave him a month's worth of lawn service to provide him with a break one summer. Then he told me about someone he knew who gave his girlfriend a blender. It just wasn't something to get excited about.

Despite my best intentions, I had clearly misjudged this one.

So I learned a few things: One, there's something special between a woman and a spa treatment. I took a poll among my friends. As I listened to their answers, I recognized how estrogen-centric spa experiences were:

Said one: "A good spa experience envelops a woman in a cocoon where someone else is in charge and tending to her, which is pretty fantastic."

Gifts: Part Two

Another said: "Spa treatments are a totally self-indulgent experience in a socially acceptable way that is renewing and offers hope that life will be more manageable."

And a third: "I love the feminine energy, the solitude, the time to center and focus on myself — the being cared for and being reminded that I need to care for my body in the very same ways I want those I love to care for theirs."

Somehow these things were all missed on my husband.

The second and perhaps most useful thing I discovered — or actually — rediscovered, was that in giving gifts, we often give ones that we would want to receive. I could have used an afternoon at the day spa. He would have been better off cycling, playing a couple of sets of tennis, or maybe even going out with his buddies for a few beers.

Next year, when it's that time again, I'm opting for no surprises. I'm going to ask my husband for a wish list — and I'm going to stick to it.

October 2000

Without a Mirror

For a jumble of reasons that I'll get to in a minute, I am living for the first time in several years without a full-length mirror in my bedroom.

Now, before you whip out the handkerchief, you should know that I only recently came to own such a household object. I was what you might call a *late-bloomer mirror-owner*.

I managed to thrive without one for the bulk of my childhood, college, post-university years, as well as through my entire first pregnancy. (I relied entirely upon photos to see my emerging mother shape.)

And I didn't have a clue as to what I was missing until I happened to see a simply designed, affordable pinewood mirror in one of those trendy local houseware stores. I didn't even stand in front of it to see my reflection — it was the shape and color that appealed. I had seen it around the time of my birthday, and when my father generously asked what was on my list of desirables, I hemmed and hawed and said, "Well, there's this mirror I have my eye on."

That's when I became a full-length-mirror owner. Once we found the right spot in the corner of our bedroom and I finally looked *in* it, not just *at* it, I was wowed. To see your *whole* self — not just you from the neck up in the bathroom mirror or from the nose on up in the car's rear view mirror or partially obstructed from the window of a public building — that was really something. Nothing quite prepared me for being able to see how a whole outfit looked, how it draped and fell on my body. This seemed to me a luxurious experience reserved for the fanciest dressing rooms of the oldest-fashioned department stores.

Without a Mirror

But the excitement of something new fades with time, right? Within just a few weeks, I was completely dependent on the thing and wondered how I ever had lived without it. I wouldn't step out of my house without that head-to-toe inspection. Wouldn't settle on an outfit unless I allowed for a proper, full-length critique. Bathroom and car mirrors sufficed no more — and forget the windows of public buildings. I was a girl who needed full-length reflection.

A few years later, when life with this full-length mirror was in full swing, my in-laws were moving and offered us their bigger, ornate oakwood mirror. So I gave away my pine one to a mirrorless friend and took on this bolder, more brazen one. It was so heavy, it took two strong men to carry it, and once it was planted in the corner of our bedroom, it stayed there without ever being moved.

That is, until recently. My in-laws were moving again, and this time, they had room in their new place for their old mammoth mirror. (Besides, it matched their bedroom furniture.)

So my mother-in-law asked if we wouldn't mind returning their mirror in exchange for a new one. (Yes, we could pick out a new one to match our bedroom furniture.)

We didn't mind and so I found another appealing mirror, this time framed in iron to match our bed. But we have been waiting for it be delivered. For almost a month now.

It has been very interesting to go back to pre-full-length days. I have found that without the chance to fuss over an outside full view, I've begun to fuss a little more over my inside. Is it a coincidence that I finally made that mammogram appointment I had been putting off, and started drinking green tea, and am back to my exercise routine? And perhaps most importantly, I'm making my clothes decisions on how it feels while I'm wearing the outfit, not necessarily on how it looks.

Could there be a connection between not having a surface reflection to stare at and starting to care more deeply within? After all, very little in the natural world provides us with a full-length view of ourselves. Not a stream or a river or an ocean or a waterfall or even a shiny stone. Was it designed this way on purpose? Perhaps we weren't meant to see ourselves reflected in living color, at full length. Maybe it's more than we ought to know and more time consuming than it ought to be.

During the time I was writing this column, the store called to tell me that my mirror was in. I could drive over there and get it today. Or I could go tomorrow, I guess. Maybe I'll pick it up over the weekend. I don't think I'm in any rush.

November 2000

Two Women and a Candle

When a young family member who lives out of town recently became seriously ill and was scheduled for a lengthy surgery and there was nothing I could physically do to help, I was at my wit's end. What can you do for a very sick child, or her family, when she lives far away? How can you possibly lend a hand?

I shared the news and my frustration with my friend Sean. I knew that she would be sensitive to the issue because she carves out time daily to pray. She and other Christian women regularly gather for prayer in one another's homes. I asked if she would pray for my little relative and Sean, who had never met the girl, generously said she would.

On the day of the surgery, I phoned Sean to let her know the time of the procedure and that's when Sean offered to pray with me. *With* me? Thoughts were racing in my head. I was thinking, *I don't know how to pray. Don't you have to be really experienced to do it right? Could we actually do it without a minister or a rabbi? And finally, would her Christian brand of prayer work with my Jewish version?*

Sean came over in close-to-emergency fashion, leaving behind her piles of work and her to-do list. She sat down with me at my dining room table. We lit the only candle I could find in the house that wasn't a Sabbath candle — a fat, vanilla-scented one — and Sean led us in prayer. She began slowly and spoke in a smooth conversational tone, nothing biblical or flowery. She spoke without any hesitation and with great confidence. Like she'd done it many times before.

Through her words, Sean took us four states away to the hospital room. She addressed the health and well-being of the doctors and nurses. *We pray they got enough sleep last night before that nothing will distract them during the procedure. That Ellen's little relative was made to feel as safe and sound as possible.* It was as if we had a movie camera and were scanning the room for details. I could *see* them. Next were the tools of the operation — she prayed that they were sterile and safe. And Sean prayed that my family could feel our support and love from so far away.

There was no choir punctuating her words. No stained glass windows shedding colorful light on hard-bound prayer books. No flowing robes or amplified voice directing our ritual. It was two women of differing faiths, a Christian and a Jew, sitting together at the table with closed eyes, praying for a child to get safely through surgery.

We must have sat together for almost an hour. Sean spoke in calming tones, the sound of her voice pacifying my worries. She'd speak, then she'd become silent. We'd meditate for a moment or two — and the longer we did this, the more I began to feel as if we were moving everything else aside and putting this little girl *first.* She deserved to be at the top of our thoughts for a while.

Hours later, we heard. To our delight, this little one came safely out of the operating room that day. This was something to truly celebrate. *Was it the prayers?* Some people believe that it is so, but we will never know for sure. But *I* was sure about a few things.

One was that even if praying didn't help my family member, it surely provided me with something constructive to do when I felt that there was nothing for me to offer. It was the first time I had ever prayed outside of a formal religious setting or without a clergy person present. Praying around my dining room table had personally connected me to my family, even though I was hundreds of miles away.

And second, this was a profound interfaith experience.

It is easy to focus on the differences between religions. But that morning, praying with Sean made me see that though our religious affiliations may help us create our rituals and understand our heritage, when it comes to sickness and health or even life and death, prayer is a powerful and universal language.

So powerful that it has had an added benefit. Ever since that June morning of our Jewish/Christian prayer effort, Sean and I have begun to talk interfaith, sharing what we know about our religions with one another. Slowly. Gently. Quietly. Carefully. We meet at restaurants, dragging our respective Bibles: her New Testament and my Tanach, or Old Testament, laden with Post-It notes and bookmarks. We have begun a tightrope walk toward better understanding one another's religious foundations. All because, as women and as mothers, we prayed together for a nine-year-old girl in Philadelphia.

December 2000

2001-2002

Whose Life?

There are two kinds of parents: Those who write about their children and those who don't.

Unfortunately for my children, I'm a parent who weaves the stories of my children's lives into essays that I share with many people on a regular basis. Every month. In big, black type.

And so it was particularly interesting for me when my daughter, who was 11 at the time, rearranged my reality and turned the tables by writing a supposedly fictional piece about a girl just about her age and a mother, who was just about mine.

It was talent night at my daughter's middle school. She had been mum about the details, telling us only that she had a short moment on stage. This wasn't too surprising, as she has spent the bulk of her after-school time in dramatics.

But that night, she sprung a new talent on the world: she could write, too. The program indicated that my daughter would be doing an original skit titled "The Birthday."

The lights went out in the cafeteria-turned-auditorium and my daughter appeared onstage under a white-hot spotlight, in the character of a middle school-age girl.

"My mother and I are having this disagreement," The Girl said, sounding surprisingly like my daughter. "We were talking about my birthday. I want three of my best friends to go to the mall with me and see an R-rated movie, and I want to stay up late. My mom, however, wants me to have the girls come over and eat popcorn and play pin-the-tail-on-the-donkey."

My mouth dropped. *Wow*, I thought, *she sure is taking on an interesting subject matter*. But why didn't she *tell* us?

Another sixth grader comes onto the stage, playing The Mom, and the two start to argue.

My face reddened in the dark. *Okay,* I said to myself, *this is fiction. And it's different for us in real life — we can talk about stuff like this.*

But the longer the staged squabble went on, the deeper my doubts. The scene sure didn't look like one from our relationship, but there she was, onstage, in public, in front of a hundred people, dramatizing a daughter who insisted that her mother was getting in the way of her desire to grow up.

The Girl sneaks out of the house, meets her friends at the mall, sees the R-rated movie, and when she leaves the theater, who does she bump into but The Mom.

The two have it out. The Girl apologizes. The Mom agrees to be more sensitive for the next birthday and concedes that her daughter is growing up. And then the stage goes black again and my daughter walks into the spotlight and concludes with a Cheshire cat grin, "My mom, she's turning out to be a pretty okay mom."

My daughter insists that this piece was not consciously written about *us*. But it was clear to me, anyhow, that I had been written about, without my permission. And I can tell you it doesn't feel very good. When her teachers approached me after the show, winking and smiling, I was, needless to say, unraveled.

But as a writer, I am also well aware of that energy that rises and refuses to settle until it is expressed. And how you look for real-life events to help illustrate your feelings and observations compellingly. How could you *not* use them?

I stewed for several days after the show, bouncing back and forth between wanting to know the truth of my daughter's intentions and not. I had been written about and it felt miserable. Eventually, I came to the only conclusion I could: I would never write about my children again.

This resolution lasted a few weeks, until the next idea hit.

And that idea was that by writing about my children, perhaps I was actually teaching them that it was okay to express oneself in a healthy, artistic way. Better this form of expression than something illegal or worse, violent.

Since then, my younger daughter has been begging me to write something new about her. I promise her that I will — I am just waiting for inspiration. Meanwhile I am secretly hoping that her favorite places under the lights remain the ice rink and the soccer field.

January 2001

Family Dinner

Ah, dinnertime. Six o'clock used to be my favorite time of the day. A chance to sit down with family or friends and let the day filter through. There is nothing quite as satisfying as lingering over a meal and settling in for the evening.

Best of all, growing up, it was someone else's job to prepare the meal. How nice to have someone fussing over you at the end of a long day. When I got older, there was usually a roommate or a partner to help. Dinner became an art form. And there was always someone else around who could help clean up.

And then I became a mother.

This meal transformed from a relaxing, expressive and nourishing time into an occasionally orchestrated but usually improvised several-act, high-energy production number. Let's face it — you've got to feed your children. But it takes effort to choose, purchase, store, prepare and serve, especially when what you really want to do is put your feet up.

Six o'clock quickly became a cherished time of the day — for my *family* — and for me, well, it just wasn't the same anymore. I'd be pulling dinner together on a weekday evening in between pick-ups and drop-offs and phone solicitations and e-mail checks and then I'd go into this fantasy:

There we are, all four of us, gathered after a long, full day for the first full meal we have as a family. I have pulled together a magnificent, healthy dinner, serving everyone's favorites with artful presentation. My husband and daughters are seated at our dining room table, speaking in soft tones, sharing bits about school, work, current events and even psychological intrigue. We talk, discuss, share, laugh, and then my children offer to clear the table and I say, "That's my girls." I'm told how deli-cious the meal was and I say, "Thank you so much for saying so," and then someone offers to rinse the dishes and put them in the dishwasher. The girls head off to their rooms to do homework and my husband and I get a chance to catch up for a few moments. Life is good.

In reality, let's just say dinner at my house is no scene from *The Waltons*. It's full of noisy and physical exchanges, behavioral ad-monitions, food criticism and lots and lots of bathroom humor. More like *The Simpsons*.

But I turned in my dinner reservations for a full-time manage-ment position in the food and entertainment industry. Dinner had lost its luster and left this mother unsatisfied.

That is, until I came across a little statistic that made me think again: There are only so many family dinners. In one year, there are about 1,000 meals. After a few skipped breakfasts and work lunches and on-the-street hot dogs and movie candy or shopping mall pizza, this leaves about 200 to 300 family meals. And what's left should be celebrated because after children leave home, all that's left is holiday meals — and holiday meals are something else entirely.

I spoke to mothers who seemed to enjoy family meals. Though each described a very different family meal, they shared one com-mon thread: they didn't serve up an agenda for dinner — just some good food and the appreciation of getting together.

I began to realize that my dinnertime fantasy had been a mas-querade for a thinly veiled expectation: that dinner should look the like meals of my youth. But my husband and children weren't there! How could they possibly be expected to reenact them? And why should they? We have our own family dinner dynamic. And if I cleared away my expectations, I might even be able to appreciate it. Bathroom humor and all.

So I have begun to practice letting go of what is supposed to happen at dinner. There doesn't have to be stimulating conversa-tion every evening. Dinner can be full of antics and good humor and may not necessarily last very long.

Family Dinner

Recently, in the middle of the week, I picked my children up from their after-school activities and ventured into the city to one of our favorite Thai restaurants. We sat down and, unsolicited, my kids began to talk about the recent presidential race and what was going on in school, and then they *mmmmed* and *ahhhed* over the food (that I didn't cook) and we had several good laughs and lots of warm exchanges. Best of all it surpassed my fantasy, because it was real.

February 2001

Yoga

A friend has convinced me to go to a yoga class with her. I think, *I don't have the time for yoga. If I'm going to start anything new, let it be a killer abs class.*

But there I am, a grown woman, lying on a rubber mat on a wooden floor with my hands on my rib cage, feeling my belly rise and fall with my breath. *This is goofy — I'm not going to burn any calories this way.* But then something happens. I become aware of how peculiar it is for an adult to be lying on the floor, just breathing. The raw, silent beauty of this experience brings me to tears. In seconds, emotion is spilling from my eyes as I lie there on the mat. *Thank goodness the mat is rubber,* I think.

How often do women stop everything and listen to their own breath? We'll marvel at a baby's breath. We listen for our child's breath over an intercom. We'll even notice the labored breath of an older, sick relative. But our own?

Other poses drew releasing tears from this newly discovered, deep inner well. Sitting on top of my legs with knees bent under, arms outstretched on the floor. Talk about a vulnerable position. Or bending over, with feet firmly grounded, arms and hands and fingers hanging loose, noticing that the tips of my fingers were getting closer to the floor.

Once I became a regular student of yoga, the weeping subsided and more loosenings took place. I reacquainted myself with soft and flexible, discovering I could bend in places that I didn't think could bend. Blood flowed, rather than meandered, through my veins. I rediscovered that I could be *gentle* and *mindful* with myself. I enjoyed this for several years.

Yoga

That was the early 1980s. Then there were pregnancies and children. My regular beloved yoga practice became an irregular one. Months and months would tick by, and conscious breathing became a distant memory rather than a practice. Triangle pose was something I'd do with my kids as we played on the floor. Warrior pose was good for waiting in line at the supermarket. Meditation was just too close to sleep. Soon yoga joined that long, growing list of really great moments from my pre-motherhood days.

Time passed and when my younger child was in first grade, another friend convinced me to go to a yoga class with her. This time, I was thinking things like, *It's too expensive; it takes too much time.* I had a list of these. But we went on a Saturday morning and I experienced my telltale tears again after a several-year hiatus. Crying never felt so good. I was back! Child posing, cat posing, dog posing, breathing, inverting, triangling. And there I've been ever since.

I have new inner dialogue about yoga; instead of critiques, it goes something like this:

Yoga is a great escape.

Yoga is cheaper than a massage.

Yoga is a way of capturing my tension and stress points and putting them on a shelf.

Yoga is a form of praying, only with the whole body.

Yoga is a way back to myself.

Now that I'm back, I've realized that I really never stopped doing yoga because even when I wasn't doing the poses, I was thinking about them. Wanting them. Craving them.

And I've come to understand why I like it so much, intellectually speaking: My yoga teacher tells us that something is yogic when it involves *stability* and *comfort.* No wonder it feels so good — how often do we feel *that?*

Yoga isn't necessarily something you accomplish like the dishes or a research project. It can feel like the first time, every time. The Buddhists talk about the beauty of the beginner's mind — that's the uniqueness of yoga. It's that every time you go, your body, your

Yoga

mind, your spirit are in a different place. Once you've gone and done a little yoga, all paths seem to lead there.

So when my mother was visiting from out of town one weekend, and I couldn't bear to miss my weekly yoga class even though she was visiting, I convinced her to join me. And to her credit, she did. Midway through the class, when all of the grown women were on the floor bent over ourselves in varying but stable and comfortable positions, my mother became very still. I stopped and scurried over to her to see if she was okay. She was okay. She looked up and that's when I saw them again: yoga tears.

March 2001

Sabbatical

Since I became a mother, my husband and I have been having an ongoing disagreement.

I say that a mother's job — no matter if she works outside or inside the home, part time or full time — is like working as actor *and* as backstage manager at a live, several-act theater production. One moment she's out there on center stage, making her theatrical magic, and then, in a flash, she's back behind the curtain undergoing a quick costume change, fixing a faulty prop, directing another actor, running to the ladies' room, rearranging someone's hair and generally trying to patch together the flow of the event in spite of endless interruptions.

As for the fathers — their days are equally full and interrupted, but if they work full time outside the home, they've got work as the main activity during the day like the actor on center stage. (Isn't the working mother most likely to get that dreaded call from the school nurse or child care provider during the day, run domestic errands during her lunch hour and sketch out dinner in her head on her way home?)

While I say a woman's day is about constantly switching hats, my husband says, *Hogwash*, he wears plenty of them. I say he gets two hours of commuting time (read: blissful transition time) in which he gets to read, rest or listen to music. He says, *baloney* — have I been on the expressways lately?

I think these stalemates with my husband are reflective of a true gender divide. A woman's life — especially a mother's — is an interrupted one, a life in pieces. Women are quick to stop what they are doing to attend to others, no matter what else is going on.

Sabbatical

Which is why I was fascinated to read a book about women who broke from convention and took a sabbatical from family life. These women, who had husbands and mostly grown children, had a dream to pursue: They went away to read the classics, engage in missionary work, teach overseas, join a dig, paint, study or write a book.

For these women, going away was about taking an adventure that would help them find their way back to themselves. Most of the women returned more self-aware, many with a clearer vision of how they wanted to live their lives.

Since reading about them, I haven't been able to get these women off my mind. I admire them for their ability to take a risk. They reminded me that there may be a time in the future, when my children are older, when I, too, might be able to arrange such a break.

But I'm suspicious about the women's reintegration into normal life. I recall how I've felt I have returned from a short sojourn. I've gone away for three-day writing retreats. I've spent long weekends with a girlfriend out of town. I've traveled away from my children with my husband. Each time I have returned refreshed, reinspired, reenergized and aching to integrate what I've learned into my daily life. And it would actually work. For about a week or two.

Then reality would set in. I'd think, *my life is nothing like it was when I had time to think or when I had transition time between events*. Might we be better off finding something in our daily life that allows us to escape for a while or dabble in a passion?

I recently read about a woman who took four months off for time to "think, play, waste and fill," after years of battling cancer. She puttered by the lake, took a motorcycle trip and generally slowed down. But she concluded that she didn't have to run away for four months to be happy. "I just need an occasional time out ... more often a few stolen moments here and there to breathe deeply and think," she wrote.

Sabbatical

For every woman who takes a sabbatical, another may be moved to make it happen for herself. This would be a good thing. But for those of us who daydream about taking one later in life; perhaps we can learn from these women. Perhaps we can move from a stage metaphor to a cinematic one. We might benefit from learning how to yell "Cut" from time to time to get a chance to breathe deeply and some time to think.

August 2001

Lessons from Mother Nature

Every morning as I leave my house and head to my car, I notice that the potted and perennial plants adding color and life to my immediate surroundings look slightly different than they did the day before.

It starts with the very first purple crocuses and red tulips in spring and goes right through the summer with the lavender petunias, orange day lilies, yellow hibiscus and red geraniums. They either show their perkiness by pointing to the sun or they never open up at all. They droop if they absorbed a big rainfall the night before or they spill over with color and leafy bushiness.

Because I'm new to this gardening thing and because I am a sucker for a good metaphor, I find myself making a connection between the daily changing shape of my potted plants to my own daily changing shape.

It feels as if my body size and shape fluctuates every 24 hours, depending on whatever wild card I've picked that day. Did I eat and what? Have I slept and how well? Have I worked the muscles recently? Did I stretch? Am I nearing my period?

Sometimes I fit into my new hipster Gap jeans and some days I need to wear my overalls from Target. Some days my underwear rides up, and other days it lies flat. Once every few months or so, I'll bravely put on a miniskirt rather than my elastic-banded balloon pants.

But I cannot seem to shake the fact that when my peonies change shape, I don't think any less of them. I am still mesmerized by their bursting bright petals and fresh fragrance. Full or limp, opened, budded or closed; leafy or skeletal, I enjoy these flowering plants. They refresh and heal merely by their existence. But even though I, too, am a beautiful creature of nature — at least according to the poets and thoughtful lovers — and my body changes are also dependent on things that are not controllable, there's *a lot* of letdown. A three-pound shift can really distract me and put a dark cloud in my day. Where did we get the idea that a living, breathing, expanding, birth-giving thing of nature should stay the same size for her lifetime, especially when clothes come in sizes 8, 10, 12, 14 and higher?

I am reminded of that time after my second child was three months old when I left her with a friend and went for a long stroll. It was January and I was covered in layers of clothes — and very aware of the extra flesh from my pregnancy.

On this wonderful winter wonderland of a walk, I noticed, since it was quiet for the first time in a long while, that I *galumphed*. I was bottom heavy. I caught my reflection in storefront windows and saw how very much space I was now taking up.

The sun shimmered on the snowcapped sidewalk and I followed the sparkles of light to the lake. As I got up close to it, I saw that the water was still and frozen, but for a few enormous ice chunks slowly bobbing along. I thought, *What a disappointment.* So gray and soundless. The lake was a sort of dirty brown dotted with icy blobs. I stared out at this strange wintry scene for a long time and after a few moments, the lake seemed to reflect back at me like a mirror. I saw myself in my post-delivery, winter-bundled state: the lake was moving slowly and bulkily. It was, galumphing along, like me. It was still grand and expansive but also in transition, hinting at spring. The ice blocks were breaking up and bouncing around in patches of moving water. It was shape shifting, like me — but nonetheless beautiful, grand and expansive. Just in transition, as women always are.

September 2001

From Nurturer to Guardian

At the park, in a store or as I was just walking down the street with my children, people whose children are grown used to stop, watch for a while and offer some variation of "How adorable! ... Enjoy them while they are young, it goes so fast ..."

I always appreciated that they said so, and I would nod and smile with gratitude. But there were many days when I thought, *Goes so fast? If you only knew how long this day felt. How many more hours until my husband comes home?*

But, as the mother of a teenager and a preteen who opt for getting dropped off places rather than voluntarily accompanying me, I think I now understand that wistful parental commentary.

It's not only that it goes fast, it's more heart wrenching than that. It's that what seemed to work before — as a parent — no longer does. How we understood our children, spoke with them and cared for them doesn't cut it anymore.

For parents in the Boomer generation, it hits doubly hard. We've tried to carve out a different way of parenting than our folks did. We struggle to comprehend our children's development. We want them to express themselves, provide them with better self-esteem, look for innovative ways to spend more time with them. We want them to be happy. We feel responsible for that. We hate it when they frown, fit or fret. We feel that there is something we can do about their "negative" feelings. A very healthy publishing industry has been built on this premise — resources our parents did not have.

The more we know and the more time we put in, the better parents we can be, right? This translates into helping to raise more whole and complete children. It makes us a unique generation of parents: We are the parents who know too much.

Those park, store and neighborhood-street parents were saying that just when you feel like you've figured out this parenting business, you ride a wave for a while and then, when you are the least prepared, everything changes. Your children enter their teens and beyond.

The things that used to connect you with your children no longer do — instead they build resentment. Questions about their day elicit nothing more than grunts, smirks or shrugged shoulders. They don't want to discuss it with *you*. That's what instant messaging is for. They've been taught to express themselves and they no longer do it on paper or canvas or on the playing field. They want to pierce their belly buttons and dye their hair Raggedy Ann red. All that encouragement doesn't necessarily fall on deaf ears, but they no longer think your opinion matters as much as peer review does.

As for general exchanges, mostly it is about what *you* can do for *them*. The one call and the sole letter we received from my daughter at camp this summer involved requests (though politely crafted) for stamps or film or snack foods, rather than descriptions of what she was doing activity-wise or socially.

It has become clear that our teenager no longer needs to be tended to in the same way as before. She tells us we make her feel overprotected, like she isn't trusted doing things for herself.

But it is an adjustment to a mother who defined herself as a nurturer. I'm a parent who used to cook a favorite meal, dispense and apply the proper medicine, readily give and receive hugs and be there to talk about triumphs as well as challenges. As parents we move from nurturers to guardians. Managers. Superintendents. There for when things go wrong. To oversee our children's general health and safety. For when things fall apart. But unlike when they were younger, there are fewer expressions of sincere thanks. Sometimes there's not a trace of appreciation whatsoever.

A parent gets the distinct impression that she won't see the results of her input for a long time. (And I thought those days back when they were little felt endless.)

Everything you ever learned about being a good parent suddenly becomes moot when it comes to your teen. You have stayed by her side all these years. Now you need to leave her be, occupy your mind with other things, but be in the next room when she comes knocking.

October 2001

A Woman's Voice

The sound of women's voices is changing, again, and though I celebrate the progress, I have a sense of what it feels like to be left behind.

When my mother discovered the women's movement back in the 1970s, her newly found voice was positively infectious. My brother and I first heard it in the excited tone she used when she asked us to heat up a frozen dinner so she could attend an evening meeting. Later, when her voice became more passionate about the subject of women and work, she became a career consultant and shared her new ideas with large groups of women. Mom used her voice fully, but I noticed that if there were face-to-face roadblocks, she would be very uncomfortable and often opt to write a letter or leave. It was a reminder that we are still a product of our time and upbringing, and she was raised without practice in navigating waves.

As for me, I stood firmly in the face-to-face express-yourself camp. It was a new era, and I utilized music and a diary to transmit my voice and I shared these with anyone who would listen. Then I went a step further and "professionalized" this desire by earning communication and journalism degrees. I was more comfortable with the uncomfortable than my mother and could say so. But I was still raised to be a good girl, so I was sure to do it sweetly and carefully for easy digestion. I had gone a step farther than my mom, but I wasn't going to cross the line into *aggressive*.

Enter the late 1990s and 2000s, — my daughters' generation. Because a woman's voice was a personal issue for me, I encouraged my girls to find and use theirs. But it was generally a moot point. They were living in a different time. Find your voice? *No problem.*

A Woman's Voice

Look for a way to express it? *Easy.* Do it publicly and effectively? *Just tell me when.* Even when they were quite young, it was clear that these girls were not only able to speak their truth, they felt *entitled* to it! And if their opinions happened to trample on someone else's truth or feelings, well, then, so be it.

They speak in public without a rehearsal or a script, voice their educated opinions on world events, pose ideas that they know are against the grain. They are comfortable questioning a teacher, calling an adult by his or her first name, making their own playdates and travel arrangements. And they are not just pleased that you would stop to listen. They insist upon it.

What a far cry from my when my grandmother was growing up at the turn of the century. She was not encouraged to speak her mind, though she had a lot on it. If my grandmother had something she wanted to say, there were times you could actually see her biting her lip. But growing up how and when she did, her way was to check in with my grandfather and run it by him first. If he shook his head *no*, she'd acquiesce. For my grandmother, men had the final word.

When my girls offer up their opinions in bulldozer fashion — and they do it often — I am torn. Though I am immensely proud of them and know that this character trait will serve them well in their future, I find that it takes energy to respond to it properly. They refuse to be dismissed. It would be so much easier if they acquiesced more. I thought most of my parenting energy would be spent in trying to support them in using their voices — not in responding or navigating around them. We have come such a long way from my grandmother's lip biting, but I see now that the women in each generation who want change can only change so much, and the women who come after can't ever really know how it felt before.

July 2002

Rest

Every summer, when my husband and daughters and I return from our family trip to my hometown, having visited grandparents, siblings, cousins, uncles, aunts and in-laws and friends, I wrestle with finding just the right words to describe it, for my own reality check.

As a working mom, I have a tendency to get excited at the prospect of leaving town. But if I call these yearly getaways *vacations*, I'll have vacation expectations — a vision of me sitting by a pool, perhaps being served something cold and frothy. I would consider calling it a break if I also didn't have to wash and fold laundry during the week or keep a restaurant server standing by while my husband answers a ringing cell phone. And *family reunion* doesn't fully describe it, either, as we usually hook up with friends or see sights as well.

It is a struggle to define because I figure if we can give our time away the right name, then perhaps we can be closer to meeting our expectations. Or rather, my expectations, which I admit are rather high: that each of us should feel like we are getting a *rest*.

I'm clearly a sucker for a challenge. For me, a rest involves sleeping in, or reading more than a page in a novel. No cooking. No laundry. For my husband, the trip gets better with every added increment of sport (doing or watching.) For my 10-year-old, it means sunshine and water. And for my teenager, well, since the whole experience is second-best to being with friends, it just has to be ... not uncool.

On these trips, we have come very close to making it work. There are obvious advantages: For one thing, we are lucky to *have* family. Second, staying with family sure does make going away more affordable. But despite these attributes, it is not what I would call ... *restful*.

Rest

During our last trip, I was curious enough to take an informal poll among the members of my family about their images of time off, of what it means to rest.

My brother-in-law said that rest was *doing nothing* although he quickly added that he wasn't very good at it, and that doing nothing usually included sleeping, reading, listening to music or drowning out the sounds of the world with his power saw. Most of which sounded suspiciously like doing something.

My aunt responded that rest meant doing something one doesn't normally do in a place one doesn't normally do it, like sewing a button in the sun or watching her grandchildren in the water.

My cousin's wife was trying to formulate her answer to my question when her six-year-old daughter burst in, curious to know what I was grilling everyone about.

So I put the question to her. "What does rest mean to you?"

"Hmmm..." she said in a serious tone. "I think that it is the feeling I have when I wake up in the morning ..."

"You mean feeling *rested?*" I asked.

"No, that's not it." Then she paused for a moment.

"I think rest is just for grownups," she offered, and ran off to join her cousins.

Of course. I had been thinking all these years that because my children work so hard at school and in their activities and because we are so scheduled during the school year, come summer, we all need down time, something different than regular life. Silly me! That *is* regular life for children. Children don't need vacations from that, but parents do!

I can't say I will stop scheduling these trips, but I think I'd get more *rest* out of them if I modified my expectations. Perhaps I'll save the word *vacation* for a precious *real* one (one where adults rule) and call *these* family events ... a *change of venue*.

August 2002

Yard Sale

I've hosted my last yard sale.

Gathering outgrown clothing, hand-me-down furniture, outdated jewelry and early-generation electronics and placing them appealingly around your driveway may be a great motivator to clear the unused stuff from your house for the chance for some extra cash, but it is a fine example of the single most effective way to bring out the worst in people. Including yourself.

Please allow me to explain.

Your intentions are good. You collect the items over the course of several weeks, checking for working parts and overall cleanliness. You haul these to the garage, stand back and mull over the objects' possible role in your future. You pick the day and turn the signs into a posterboard-and-marker-project for your 10-year-old daughter and her friend. You arrange for your kids to each bring a friend to help for a percentage of the earnings — the teenage one sleeps over the night before to ensure waking up before noon. You agree to let your younger daughter set up a lemonade stand. And the Weather Channel reports clear skies ahead.

But the morning of the sale, crime, dishonesty and greed prevail.

Just as you are staple-gunning your handmade posters around the neighborhood, a police officer informs you that you are breaking beautification laws and that you'll have to tear them down and place them on your own property. This would not have been so devastating if you had put an ad in the paper, but you didn't because the last time you did that, it cost $35 and the ad never ran.

Yard Sale

It takes four tries, but finally your children/helpers awake. Younger sister is caught admiring older sister's T-shirt as clothing is laid out on an aluminum folding table. Younger sister asks if she can have it as a hand-me-down. Older sister says she will have to buy it until peer pressure from her friend (who is herself a younger sister) convinces her to let younger sister have it.

Your husband, who said he would be happy to help, takes a bike ride that morning and manages to get home in time for the rest of the Tour de France on TV.

Younger sister is keeping tabs and growing upset that older sister has made more money despite the fact that older sister had more to sell, but nothing you say is helping her understand this.

A small flurry of cars pulls over. You sell your grandmother's gaudy gold mirror for $15 less than your bottom line. You sell your in-laws' Mickey Mouse phone, even though they asked you not to. You feel slightly guilty about this. Your neighbor comes over with her three-year-old and she picks out some books and figurines. You really want to give these to her — after all, they just moved to the neighborhood — but you promised to pay something to your kids. So you reluctantly charge them the $3.50. You feel bad about this later.

There is very little traffic. You wonder if you should have sprung for the newspaper ad. You call a local charity so that a truck will come to pick everything up the following week. You consider giving the stuff away. And then you do. Your cousins come over and you convince them that the leather recliner would look great in their basement.

As you pack everything up, you notice that you are dragging almost everything back in that you brought out in the morning. A passerby tells you that a giant church rummage sale was taking place just a few blocks away.

You do a little mental accounting. You have been working on this project for weeks. The day's tally comes to $119 plus change. After you take away the cost of the eight posterboards and the lemonade and the cups and your help, you have $39. You wonder if you should put it in your savings account. You consider giving it to charity. But you conclude that it would be just enough for dinner out, because you are way too tired to cook.

This fourth — and final — yard sale has provided me with a new motto:

If a thing we own has outgrown its usefulness, it should not have to serve us again by earning us money. Commerce should be kept separate from housekeeping. So, in a few years, when things begin to accumulate again, I'm thinking we will bypass the kiosk pit stop in the driveway, take the stuff directly to charity and allow the things to find their karmic purpose, without the sound of change jingling in our pockets.

September 2002

Nose Piercings

My 14-year-old daughter, Emily, has two pierced holes in each of her ears. She has been vying for one for her nose. We have had numerous conversations that have prompted me to ponder why a young woman would actually choose to adorn herself in this way. And I have a theory with which Emily disagrees. I thought it might be interesting to converse in print on the topic, so here is our conversation, as it went.

Mom: I can understand the desire to poke a hole or two in each ear and slide attractive art objects through them. I've got two myself and Grandma Joyce has got four. But why a nose ring?

Emily: Okay, granted I do have more than my fair share of holes in my head. A nose ring symbolizes much more than just a piece of art. Dating all the way back to ancient India, women wore nose jewelry as a celebration of womanhood. I've also read that it is supposed to help relieve menstrual discomfort and the pain of childbirth.

Mom: Sounds like you've done your homework, and clearly you've thought a lot about this, but let's be real here — we're in the Midwest, not India.

Emily: Americans have always imported their habits from all over the world, so why should a nose ring be any different?

Mom: Good point. But I have another theory about why teens are taking this practice to the extreme. I think that maybe all of that metal is like wearing a form of armor to protect you in these unpredictable times.

Nose Piercings

Emily: *Mom*, I really doubt that teenagers are even subconsciously trying to arm themselves, especially in these horribly dangerous Midwest suburbs.

Mom: I do have another theory. I think that teens are looking for their own version of a rite of passage — something like an aborigine walkabout or a spiritual retreat — where they survive the pain and then have something to show for it.

Emily: And what, exactly, is wrong with that?

Mom: Well, isn't life painful and hard enough as it is to do something like that on purpose?

Emily: People I have spoken with who have had their nose pierced say it isn't painful at all. Trust me, we're not masochists. A nose piercing is different than any other kind. It's made of the same stuff your upper ear is, cartilage. Therefore, anyone who's ventured to get his or her cartilage pierced shouldn't expect anything more painful than that. A tongue piercing is muscle, a belly ring is skin, but it is in a very sensitive spot. An eyebrow ring is in an even more delicate place where it's easy to get ripped out. Other piercings, which sound too painful to even discuss, well, they're obviously something one does at their own risk and pain threshold.

Mom: Okay — lets' steer away from the pain issue because clearly it is subjective. Why would a nose ring bring you pleasure? Why do you feel you need it to feel or look more beautiful than you already are?

Emily: Why did I want to get my ears pierced? Why did I want to dye my hair pink? I guess in all honesty it was partly for the reaction, but I've moved past caring so much what everyone thinks and expects me to be. Right now, it's more about how I feel about myself. Being a teenage girl is hard enough. Before, I was constantly looking in the mirror and disliking what I saw. Now I feel that way less, which must be a sign that all these seemingly rebellious acts have helped in some way. I really can't say for sure what it is about a nose ring that appeals to me, but what I do know is that every time I see one, I get uber-jealous and want one of my own because I find it so attractive. I've always been told to accentuate the positive and eliminate the negative, but in this case, how about I just adorn myself?

Mom: I hear you, Em. I have often thought that today's nose rings are being seen by my generation like long-haired boys were viewed in the '60s.

Emily: Good. Now that we understand each other, can I just get the nose ring?

Mom: Would you consider a belly ring?

Emily: Well, I guess that'll do.

November 2002

Postscript: Soon after this discussion, Emily got her belly button pierced. It became infected within a week and she let it close up. A few months later, she opted for a nose piercing (without parental consent), which she proudly wears to this day. Eventually, her mother got over it.

The Annual Family Photo

December is the time of year that people like to express themselves by snail mail.

The choices are overwhelming. There's the charitable or brand-name holiday greeting card. There's the glossy photo of the children — or the dog — inserted into a card with a built-in frame. There's the year-in-summary letter. There's the homemade card. The electronic card. Electronic card with attached digital photo.

My favorite holiday greeting to send, and to receive, is the annual family photo copied onto card stock with a pithy sentiment typeset inside. What's not to like about opening an envelope to see friends or family members as they change hair, height or haute couture?

Every year, from late summer to late fall, each photograph that is taken of my husband, daughters and me is a candidate for the cover of our card. There's the Barish family on a dock as the sun is setting by the ocean. Under a tree in an apple orchard. Dressed in new outfits for the Jewish High Holidays. Seated around an immense pumpkin. In a backyard hammock. If the selection isn't so good that year, we go to the nearest tree, woods or sculpture park to set some photos up.

For amateur pictures taken by my husband, who sets the timer and runs into position, they aren't half bad, so I'm told. Some friends tell me that they save the cards in their photo albums. This is nice to hear. Especially because I know what it took to get it.

See, behind the smiling faces of my children and my husband and me, blood is boiling. A few years ago, a camera's lens used to mean the chance to ham it up and beam to make Mom smile. Now that my daughters are 11 and 14, self-consciousness rules and pleasing a parent in such an easy way is no longer a worthwhile goal. Add to this the fact that I am a perfectionist about the photo's quality and that neither of these lovely young women is ever pleased with the outcome, and you might understand why there's resistance. Which makes it extremely difficult to get a good shot.

But where family photos are concerned, I am a woman obsessed. During the shoot, this translates into all manner of promises and negotiations, all the while my husband standing by, allowing me directorial creativity (which he claims is closer to dictatorial creativity) and my daughters looking at their watches, saying, "Do we have to take an entire roll, Mom?" or "I don't like this position" or "Are we done yet?" It is a delicate procedure to insist on cooperation from a group who would rather be anywhere else while simultaneously keeping tempers in check to save the photo.

Afterwards, everyone trots off in a huff in different directions to cool down. And when a finalist is selected and the cards are made and ready for their mass mailing, someone is unhappy. Someone's face is partially obstructed. Someone's hair isn't just right. Someone's expression is off. Sometimes there are even tears. And this is far from a pretty picture.

So the truth is that every member of my family detests the experience.

Except me, of course. I am unbending about this annual ritual and will probably continue to be until we no longer live together as a family. I'm thinking of it as an investment, banking on the idea that later — much later — these photos, which hang framed on the wall in our living room might be considered valuable property long after I'm gone.

It is a thankless job to be the family photo archivist, but those of us who are don't do it for the thanks.

December 2002

2003-2004

Letting Go, Again

Some time ago, I had an instinct that something wasn't okay with my older daughter, emotionally speaking. I was worried enough to take an aggressive parental step — one that I weighed carefully before taking — but one that I hope you don't ever have to take.

I read my daughter's diary.

To give you a sense of how dreadful this was for me, I should confess that I am a life-long journal keeper. I have stacks of them in numerous boxes stored in my house. They contain more than 30 years of personality profiles, soap-operatic stories, teary losses, counting of blessings, future plans, to-do lists, article ideas and, of course, descriptions of constantly changing feelings. I consider these pages to be my rocks, my stepping stones, the best inanimate friends a woman can have.

I knew that both of my daughters wrote their thoughts and feelings down from time to time in diaries with inefficient little locks on them. When the girls were old enough to understand about public and private places, our family policy was this: Whenever you found yourself in someone else's room — to borrow a shirt or to put a pile of folded laundry on the bed — you were to steer clear of the pages you might see lying on the bedside table. The diaries were off limits.

The day I crossed that line — that line a caring parent sometimes has to cross so that she can sleep at night — the policy maker had become the policy breaker. I read the pages of my daughter's diary through a torrent of tears.

A few days later, once I gathered my strength, I came clean. I shared with my daughter what I now knew in as calm a fashion as I could muster. She was 13 at the time and understandably mortified. It took some time to rebuild the trust that was lost between us that day. Though it was one of the most horrible moments of my mothering life, I believe it was the right thing to do: It allowed me the opportunity to provide her with the help she needed.

I'm reminded of this incident because I recently felt that urge to look again. Not because I was as worried as I was before — it's very different now. There wasn't that sense of emergency that I had so many moons ago. The desire to search through her diary was more like a compulsion to quickly glean what was going on in her head so I could just be *sure*. So I'd feel like I had some *sense of control*. After all, it was readily available source material.

And I almost went for it. While she was at school, I got as far as her bedside table and spied where her journal sat. I recalled how just a few years before, reading the words she put onto the page felt like a form of rescue. But on this particular day, with only generalized concerns behind the desire to check in and see how things were going, I realized that what I was about to do was indeed an invasion. Back then, reading her journal was part of the fix for my daughter, but in this moment, it was more like a fix for Mom. I took hold of myself and walked out of her room.

After that close encounter with my daughter's diary, I remembered the first day that I forgot to ask the babysitter what my daughter ate while I was away. It was anxiety producing and freeing at the same time. Then there was her first full day of school; her first sleepover; my first full week away from her on vacation. We had survived these firsts. And though this teenage version seemed far weightier, I knew that these prior firsts were intimately linked to this one. My daughter was going to have experiences — and feelings — that I was not going to be privy to, and we would both survive it.

I recently saw an old episode of *The Simpsons* in which Lisa, the middle of three children and a precocious second grader, is feeling blue. She doesn't know why and doesn't really want to talk about it. Mother Marge is worried but advises Lisa to smile and never let the world know how she really feels because it is easier that way — and besides, that's how Marge had been raised. Following her mom's advice, Lisa is overwhelmed with insincere attention from her classmates upon arriving at school with her smile pasted on. Marge watches from the car, sees the danger in this, and re-advises Lisa to be herself, even if it means that Lisa is sad. Though Marge never finds out what is making Lisa feel that way, Marge allows Lisa to have these privately sad feelings without judgment. The important thing is that her family will stand by her, however long it will take to move on from sad.

What a complex relationship a mother has with her growing child. We can either choose to fret over what we don't know, or let go. Because controlling our children is an illusion, but having an influence on them is an art.

April 2003

High School Hopes

Until recently, I could count as one of my parental blessings that my children liked academics and that they fared well in this pursuit.

Then my older daughter entered high school.

The first semester went as we were accustomed. (Good grades are easy to get used to.) But in the second, certain letters of the alphabet that I was not used to seeing began to show up on those mid-term grade reports. And by the last set of grades — *yeow* — her profile made me wonder if she had swapped her brain with someone else, like she trades T-shirts and jeans.

I was not pleased. In my mind, my teenage daughter had developed good study habits over the years, a sense of academic confidence, and nothing was preventing her from getting good marks.

She'd pled, "High school is much harder than middle school, Mom, you don't understand." Oh, I understood, all right: *she was goofing off.* Letting it all slide. I was already fast-forwarding to college. I wanted her grades to reflect how smart I knew her to be so she could have choices. Groundings and earlier curfews were instituted. I would not be budged.

It's interesting that during that time, I forgot about an academic blip of my own. There was a period in middle school, right around the time that all those standardized tests began to loom, that my grades, which hovered at slightly better than average for most of my career but were certainly not stellar like my daughters', turned. It all stemmed from a reading comprehension problem. The essence of a paragraph wouldn't be clear to me. I'd have to read it several times before I could get its main point.

It got bad enough to merit tutoring. I met with my tutor, reluctantly and clandestinely, and told no one. (Academic excellence was held in high regard at my house and it seemed to me that I was falling short.) I was lucky not to have a physical limitation. I was not dyslexic. My eyesight was fine. I was not haunted by headaches. I've since concluded that during this period I was simply distracted. Other things seemed more important to me than tests and grades — things like social status and romance and daydreams and those big life questions.

Remember having the time for those?

But no memory of this came to me as my daughter's grades took a downward spiral. I reacted with fear and threats.

Academics are important and dang it, I was not going to let her throw her hard work away. So instead of offering understanding or options, I handed her my displeasure and my criticism and if-thens and lots of advice that went in one ear and out. This was a very non-productive thing to do.

But good mothers who don't see results try other approaches, right? Two, to be exact. And thankfully, more productive ones. I called my daughter's teachers and her dean. We met. They were not overly concerned given her academic record, but they recommended that my daughter go in after school for extra assistance. She did some extra work here and there and ultimately rethought her course load for sophomore year with her counselor.

Second, with the school staff behind me, I worked on relaxing a little and waiting, which can be very difficult for a mother.

But it was during this time that my own academic memories resurfaced. I remembered feeling antsy in the hard wooden seat during those sunny spring afternoons in a small, one-windowed office with my reading tutor. I remember how she helped me break down a paragraph. I remember seeing for the first time how a series of sentences, depending on their structure and word choice, could evoke emotion in a reader. I remember the flicker of lights going back on in my head and, eventually, my grades beginning to pick up.

And that's when I realized that I have yet another parental blessing: my own experience. Though grades are a reasonable predictor of success — whatever that may mean — a perfect linear relationship does not exist between the two. After all, I was a girl with reading comprehension challenges who ultimately came to make her living with words. Looking back at my own academic twists and turns was a reminder to keep the long range in view, though I will admit, that I have higher hopes for next year.

August 2003

A Pregnant Pause

I am surrounded by women who are about to become mothers, and as I watch them prepare for their new title — the one they know will change everything but with no clue as to how — I have a newly discovered appreciation for that small pocket of time right before a woman becomes a mother.

My sister Katie tell tales of wacky food cravings and aversions. I watch her grapple over paint colors for the baby's room. I nod when she tells me that pregnancy hormones feel like natural anti-depressants. I am remembering feeling these things too and having the time to mull over them.

My friend Nancy is adopting a toddler from a country so far away that it will take two days to get there. She took the time before Gracie's arrival to undergo a surgery that she'd been putting off. I think of her recovery time and her long flight as her version of gestation and delivery. Painful, involving a hospital and rest, and time to think and take stock, like so many of us experience prior to becoming moms.

My neighbor Renee is pregnant with twins. She and her husband, Tom, are building a huge addition on their home. She is on partial bed rest now and goes to her parents' house when she can to get away from the noise and construction. She's shopping for adorable outfits for the babies and, of course, for herself, and I am remembering the joy in that.

As I observe these women doing the groundwork for an entirely new role, I am reminded of how this time frame, right before a woman becomes a mother and just before she is forever transformed, is completely unique. It never happens again. How brilliant nature is for granting women time before this overwhelming change. How useful all that paperwork and red tape is for women to wade through before they become mothers through adoption.

So much to gain — and, of course, lose.

It's the last time these women will ever be able to put themselves *first*. The final stretch where their aches and pains can be attended to before their baby's. The conclusion to living their lives as Katie, Nancy and Renee without the title of *mother*. Decisions are now made with the possibility of impacting another's person's life — more so, I think, than a spouse or roommate. They are soon to be someone's mom.

Watching them and hearing about their experiences has been stirring up memories of what I did before becoming Mom. During those last months before my first daughter was born, I spread out collected sick days. I took Fridays off so that I'd have long weekends to nest-build and go to a pregnancy yoga class and just relax. I spent a lot of time with friends. I took a lot of photos of my puffed-up belly. I studied baby names. I read a lot. I slept a lot. I journaled a lot. Ate a lot. Dreamt a lot. Shopped a lot. Got fussed over. I was not anxious or worried — I felt like my sister did, that the hormones of pregnancy protected me somehow. I was carrying a bigger and more important weight. I remember my pregnancy as a magnificent journey.

If you detect a bit of wistful longing, you are not mistaken. Once that weight is delivered into the world, or in my friend Nancy's case, swooped up and brought home on an airplane, that window in time shuts and the woman she was before she was a mother is now gone. She's hardwired into her new mother role and can be brought back through memory.

This seems a particularly poignant change if, like the women who surround me now, they move into motherhood later in life. These women have loved, worked, earned graduate degrees, traveled, sold and bought homes — they have lived a full life being able to put their desires first. Overnight — or via a long-distance flight — a woman who has just become a mother shifts into focusing on a tinier and needier creature than herself. The work of pregnancy — or the paper trail of the adoption process — has given her some of the tools to weather all sorts of atmospheric pressures. The others come from this quiet before the active weather system that is motherhood.

I wonder, is this period what is really meant by a pregnant pause? A break in the proceedings, a hiatus on life, before a woman moves into motherhood — a brief but necessary building block inspired by nature for a woman who seeks the name *mother*.

November 2003

A Woman and Her Handbag

I'm not a collector by design, but I believe I may be one because of it. The design of women's handbags, that is.

Like many women I know, I suffer the predicament of the pocketbook. The crisis of the clutch. Hell in a handbag.

I've accumulated enough of these attractive little containers — woven, straw, rope, beaded, vinyl, velvet, leather and linen — to open a small boutique. I've got backpacks, fanny packs, carriers and totes. They strike me as well designed when I'm looking at them in the store. But once I bring them home, I quickly discover a multitude of impracticalities.

Like that soft red-brown leather wallet that is attached to a shoulder strap but has no place for a cell phone. Or the multicolored latchless straw bag into which you could fit two hardback books but is too tempting for a thief. Or the black vinyl and leather rectangular sack with a pouch inside that hangs to mid-thigh with an unadjustable strap. Or the fanny pack that won't fit under certain coats.

Is there such a thing as a perfect purse?

Last summer, a friend presented me with a shoulder bag that came as close to ideal as I thought a bag could be. It was made of soft, pliable weatherproof material. It was about a hand and a half big. Squarish. Gray and black. It had a front flap containing a place for credit cards and checkbook. There were no internal pockets, but there was an attached change purse and a cell phone pouch.

But with it came an unforeseen design flaw: As small as it was, it was too deep: Once I went digging into it, digging is all that I did.

A Woman and Her Handbag

Since I've been traveling more and needing to take my life with me on the road, I've concluded that the trauma of the tote and the burden of the bag is a woman's issue.

While men have the battle of the bulge — pocket bulge, that is — women, especially mothers, have few options for something that is small enough and light enough not to stiffen our necks or cramp our wrists; large enough to carry the grocery store receipts, field trip notices, basketball schedules and birthday party invitations, as well as weather-proof and something we might call *good looking.*

Retailers may promote purses as accessories, but to most women these containers are more than mere attachments. They are the holder of our cash, checkbooks, credit cards and cell phones. They hold the necessities of life. Kleenex. Lip balm. Gum. Change. Coupons. Datebook or electronic organizers. Comb. Aspirin. And an assortment of other womanly needs.

I've tried to go without. I experimented one week by walking around like men do, with cash and a credit card tucked into a billfold in my pocket. That was the time I lost my cash card. I had a go at the wallet concept. No place for my datebook. I've gone the other way, carrying around the equivalent of a child's backpack. All I can say about that is, *Oy, my aching back.*

There seems to be no way around it: The perfect purse does exist, but not for long. A woman's handbag is designed for short-lived service. The best bag is one that's customized to the event. The trip to the grocery store. A business meeting. An evening out. Maybe, if she's lucky, she can utilize the same bag all day long. But that beaded clutch is just not going to cut it at Costco. And that leather backpack will make a back sweat in the summer heat.

This seems a familiar refrain for women's lives: that a woman's handbag serves a woman's life, a life chopped up into different pieces. A woman's bag might be a metaphor for how a woman must stay flexible, willing to transfer life's necessities from one container to the next, hoping desperately that important stuff won't get lost in the shuffle.

A woman's carry-all bag may indeed be a symbol, but I think I just rationalized my next purse purchase.

January 2004

What She Lives For

NOTE: *Several years ago (July 1998), after my kindergarten-age daughter would not let up over her desire to enter a skating competition, I pondered the wisdom of allowing her to compete at such a young age. Now, six years later, Jenny Rose, 12, tells us, in her own words, why it means so much to her. And now, I understand.*
— EBB

For the fourth consecutive year, I would be skating in my ice rink's competition. I had a reputation at the arena for being the little girl with short legs who could really put on a show. This year, I would be skating to Michael Jackson's "Thriller." I had just learned to land my axel but like all skaters, the mental games got in the way and I wasn't always consistent.

The morning of the event, I awoke in a cold sweat. I had spent that night obsessively going over my routine in my head. It would have to be flawless. My dress — the velvety black one with blue gems on the chest, the one that my grandmother had bought for me months before — was laid out on my chair. Most importantly, I would wear the signature M.J. white glove.

My grandma put layers and layers of makeup on me and my mom gave me Princess Leia buns (which were pulled way too tight and giving me a terrible headache). I hoped that the pain would pass. This wasn't working, so I decided to just breathe and get my skates on. Now another unpleasant feeling met my body. It felt heavy, like some gravitational force was pulling me down. Nerves.

My mom offered me a drink, but I just couldn't handle the extra substance in my stomach. My coach approached me and made a frantic signal.

"It's time to sign in! You have 15 minutes."

Nerves came on like a tidal wave that nearly knocked me over. It was that same feeling that I experienced at this very moment every competition: the feeling that your stomach could explode at any given moment because of the overcrowding of butterflies. The stands were filling. My cheering section yelled my name.

The time between a competitor's turn to skate and another competitor is about the longest five minutes in a skater's life. My coach urged me not to watch the other skaters, because comparing was not the best thing to do before you compete. If you overthink it, you blow it. For the twentieth time, I did my mental checks — when to kick my leg and where to sway my arms. I heard the audience's applause, meaning a performance had ended and mine would soon begin. All that I had been anticipating came down to this very moment. I could not depend on my coach, my mom or my dad; I had to depend on myself.

I gracefully glided to the center of the ice and presented myself to the audience. I was going to kill this thing. I positioned myself in my first pose and just let myself go. My camel spins soared through the air, and when I landed my axel, I was exuberant! Every muscle in my body was put to work and every dance move was given a Jenny Barish flair. I was unstoppable.

When my solo was nearing an end, my stomach started to lurch. My throat was dry, my eyes began to water and my head was spinning. All that was left was a smile and a pose. I went into my scratch spin and my body gave out. It was over. I slowly got up, fanned myself, and signaled to my coach that I wasn't feeling so well.

Too late.

I knew that nerves on an empty stomach would not be a good mixture. From that day on, I was known as the girl who threw up at the competition, all over the floor. *Great.* I thought my chances for a win were shattered.

What She Lives For

I scanned the score sheet and found my name, double checking to make sure what I saw was really there. A few spaces to the right of my name was the number one! My family and friends gathered by me where I announced my triumph. I made my way to the award table, where I took my first-place trophy. Although it was just a cheap hunk of plastic, it stood for more than that. It stood for flaws. Because of this whole ordeal, I learned that things may not go as planned, and that you should be prepared for the unexpected.

I know what you are about to ask: Why do I put myself through such a physical and emotional roller coaster? The answer is simple: Stress, triumph and victory are just the kind of things I live for.

Jennifer Rose Barish
February 2004
Age 13

Home Office Window

There once lived a woman whose house was not just where she lived, but also the place in which she made her living.

On the first and second levels of this two-story 1950s Colonial in the suburbs, the woman cooked, cleaned and cared for her two children. On the lower level, below ground, in a partially finished, mildewy basement with dark faux wood paneling, disintegrating linoleum and a window that did not open, she word-smithed, punctuated by the laundry room sounds of water sudsing and clothes thumping.

Despite the olfactory and visual challenges, the woman felt blessed to be able to close a door to transform herself from mother-wife-homemaker into writer-editor-business owner. She worked steadily, wrapping her work schedule around the pace of her children's lives.

And for a long time, it was good.

Until the assignments dwindled and the time between them expanded. When the projects did materialize, they appeared similar to the ones before, but with different client names and e-mail addresses. Despite her best efforts, she could not lure in a new and interesting workload.

Around this time, her children's needs were shifting. They required more rides, but they no longer had to be reminded to do their homework. Her children were more interested in the world away from home and had become somewhat responsible for themselves.

As a consequence of this change, the floors of the woman's home fell silent. And with her work down to a slower pace, she thought that she had been lucky for a good run, but that perhaps it was now over — that she should be pleased, but prepare to pack it on up. And this made the woman very sad, indeed.

Home Office Window

She began to think that mothers of a certain age were no longer useful to their children, except for the last-minute lifts and dollar dispensations. She worried that it might be true in the business world. Maybe the world was more interested in women of a younger age, the ages of her daughters, and it made the woman feel as if she was fading into the background just a little.

One summer day in the midst of this period — with one child away at summer camp and the other one working a part-time job — the woman decided to clean out her office in the basement. She sorted files and boxes and correspondence, and moved the pieces of her office temporarily into a second-floor bedroom.

This bedroom had been empty except for a television and a couch. In it was a window that could open, unlike the small, underground rectangular piece of glass in the basement. As she fingered the papers of her working life, she opened this window to let fresh air in. In that moment she noticed that while she worked, daylight was shining in, a July breeze was blowing and birds were tweeting. And this was very good.

It was so good that the woman proposed to her family that she make it a permanent move. To her surprise, no one quarreled.

And that's when the balances shifted and her work and home life changed. New projects materialized at such a pace that the woman had to very reluctantly let some go. These career-stretching assignments asked her to reach back into her arsenal of knowledge, mixing it in with what she knew now, which energized her place in the outside-of-home working world. Her children barely noticed the difference — they were entrenched in their own lives.

Interior designers might consider this change *better feng shui*. Office designers might even claim it to be *better ergonomics*. But the woman, who was also a mother and a writer and an editor, thought that perhaps she had simply, finally, moved her talents into the light, with some fresh air to blow away the dust and a chorus of birds to root her on.

March 2004

Other Mothers

Whatever would I do without other mothers?

Who better than mothers with children older than mine to talk to about getting through the tough times — aren't they living proof?

Who else but a mother can fully relate to operating for months at a time on naps and continually interrupted work — not to mention all that happens to our physical and mental health in the process?

Who else but another mother would stay on the telephone with me in the wee hours of the morning until our teenagers got safely home?

This is not to say that other fathers don't enter into the picture. I know one dad who makes all of the Hebrew school carpool arrangements. Another is the grownup home after school when the girls hang out together. And my own husband is the soccer coach.

Nor am I saying that other folks and communities aren't in the picture, as ours was recently one that helped a school referendum pass.

No, I'm not denying that it truly takes a village to raise a child. It's just that I believe that it is other mothers who can create a powerful circle of support around us if we let them. A conversation with another mother — even on the run in the grocery or school parking lot — can be a source of strength when we are hanging by a thread. Sharing our stories can remind us that we really have a complex management position in the family business.

I saw my first glimpse of this other-mother factor during a Lamaze class 16 years ago. It was the first time I found myself in a group of women with whom I was connected by something other than school or work or neighborhood alone. It was understated then, we'd connect with a glance or, during a breathing exercise, a grimace. But there was no doubt that these were women in my community with whom I was about to deliver a new generation.

At my first mothers' group, I shared and learned tidbits about the latest toys and books and tools of our new trade. Meeting with these women provided me with pre-selected recommendations — ones with weight behind them.

When we moved to our house, four pregnant women lived on the block. Neighbors with same-aged children are more than worth their weight in gold. There's nothing like opening the side door to the house and letting your youngster walk over to the next-door neighbors' backyard swing set, knowing that a mother is watching from her kitchen window, as are you from yours.

Once my children entered preschool and elementary school and formed friendships, another surprise from other mothers: they became incredibly valuable for learning more about my children — outside of home. We could discuss what occurred at playdates and we'd troubleshoot when we needed to.

Now that my children are in middle school and high school, I have hit the mother lode when it comes to other mothers. The stakes are bigger now — we don't worry so much over skinned knees or lack of sharing but about car accidents and substance abuse. So when our teenagers aren't answering their cell phones, we can contact one another and see who was last in touch, and when. If things get really out of hand, then we can share information and decide communally on consequences, as a force of many rather than one.

Years ago I attended a gathering of women in which our guides were two women who had reached grandmotherhood. It was designed as a day devoted to mothers, facilitated by mothers. In between three lovely meals, we sat in a circle, told some of our family stories, collaged, stretched, listened to music and journaled.

We also questioned, meditated, giggled and cried. When I left, I carried the sense that I was truly a link of a chain — circles connected to circles within a circle — and that I was in no way, shape or form alone in this. Though I haven't kept in regular touch with the women from that circle, I still feel supported by them; it is enough knowing they are out there as I am, having good days along with the not-so-good ones.

Perhaps as we raise the children, it's other mothers who are raising us.

May 2004

She Drives

How can it be?

Just yesterday she had a check-up at the pediatrician's office.

The day before, while delivering a pile of clean laundry to her room, I found her beloved stuffed puppy dog in between pillows on her bed.

And the day before that, she flashed her metal-capped teeth and requested a special utensil to brush in between her braces.

And now, she drives.

She's had the lessons. Completed all the hours behind the wheel. Passed the driving school written exam. The state has her name in the computer system.

All that's left is setting up the car insurance and the actual trip to the motor vehicle department for the driving test. But to tell you the truth, I've been putting these off.

I don't know what's crazier, really — me staving off a 16-year-old who has completed all the steps necessary to start an engine and drive into the sunset or that someone, somewhere, at some time decided that 16-year-olds could drive.

After all, teenagers are the quintessential multi-taskers. Highly distractible. Cell phone-centric. Prone to offering rides to numerous friends and paying attention to inside-the-car conversations rather than outside-the-car obstacles.

They drive too fast down narrow suburban streets. They drive too slowly on the expressways. And they need to practice when you've got to get somewhere fast. (I've been recalling those days when she was a toddler and she was aching to help vacuum or stir cookie batter and I knew it would take triple the time but I had to stop, take a breath and remind myself that time and a tidy job didn't matter — what mattered most was her experiences doing these things ... and of course, keeping my patience in check.)

But that's carpeting and cookies, and this is life and death.

Yes, I know. We were all new drivers once. It takes a while to become one with the wheel. To collect enough experiences to gain confidence on the road.

But my daughter earning a driver's license is, for me, scarier than most of the milestones before it.

Scarier than when she first learned how to walk, because there wasn't that far to fall.

Scarier than her first bike ride around the neighborhood, when I knew the parameters and could watch from the windows.

Scarier than when she first boarded a downtown train by herself because we had carried on a step-by-step cell phone conversation for the entire first trip.

However competent she will ultimately become as a driver, I won't always be there to intervene, to react to the mistake that the other guy makes. And there's no chance whatsoever that I can watch from the window or know the lay of the land or talk to her by cell phone (unless she's stopped the car first). No, that's probably the thing: there is no me at all in this picture — just my 16-year-old and everyone else on the road at that moment.

And this provides the mother of the new driver with choices: Develop an ulcer? Have an anxiety attack? Start drinking? Anything to numb the horrific side effect of parenting a teenage driver: fear.

Or — and I'm not saying this is so easy — perhaps a parent can try on something I'll call faith. If a parent didn't have any before, she might very well consider trying it on for size at this juncture. Because what other good option is there? Ulcers are painful. Anti-anxiety medication can get pricey. And drinking, well, a lot of good that would do me if she ever needed me to come and get her.

She Drives

Truth is, when I cringe or gasp or yelp or cajole or correct or even sit in the front seat and silently stew, my daughter doesn't drive very well. When I experimented recently by sitting in the back seat, she was better. More relaxed. On her game. She noticed it, too, and said, "Mom, when you yell at me, I lose it. I drive better with Dad because he's calmer."

I guess this isn't too much of a surprise. But compelling. I suppose fear is palpable, sniff-able. Lack of faith in her ability is possibly dangerous.

So I'm giving it a shot.

June 2004

2003-2004

The Orchid

As I sit on this rickety, metal-spined office chair trying to get comfortable so that I can write, a woman I've known and loved without even the tiniest break since the day I met her is struggling to find just a few small, pain-free moments from a wheelchair in a rehabilitation hospital four states away.

I ache to see her. To put my arms around her. To hand-deliver flowers or sushi. To massage her feet. To sit beside her and listen to whatever she may want to say, or to her silence. To clean her house. To take her sons to the movies.

The things we do out of deep friendship. For those special friends — the ones we met on the seventh-grade camping trip, when it rained all weekend and we slept beside one another under a dripping nylon tarp, bonding over how uncomfortable we were.

Just like now. Uncomfortable.

But for the past several weeks, for as long as she has been sick, my treasured buddy has been declining my offers to board a plane and come to her side. I make arrangements to travel to her, but she says it's all she can do to get through her rehabilitation and then spend time with her husband and sons. She's been through hell and she's only just beginning to recover her strength. She needs time to process all of this. She'll call when she's ready.

Come later, she says, *when I'll need you more.*

I understand this, of course. It makes sense. But nothing is staying sensible for long right now. This came over her suddenly and turned her life upside down — what's logical about that? I hate that I can't do anything for her. Every muscle in my body wants to act. Isn't it through our actions that we show our love?

The Orchid

I want to bake. To do laundry. To carpool her children. To weed her garden. To urge her husband to go for a walk. I'd even make a casserole, and I don't cook.

Other than praying, which is becoming an everyday ritual offering some solace and temporary calm, what is a heartbroken friend to *do* with all of her *doing* energy?

I leave messages of support on my friend's cell, home answering machine and in her e-mail box.

I send cards and compact discs, poetic verses and comedy DVDs, and a cozy shawl, in turquoise.

And for a day or so, it feels like *something*.

A few weeks into this long-distance crisis, on a whim, while in a flower shop considering sending flowers to her, I surprise myself by bringing an orchid home. It was in every respect, uncharacteristic. I'm not gifted with plants. I have never bought an orchid before, nor has anyone given me one. I find them so delicate, so intimidating, so high maintenance. It was purple and fuschia — about two-thirds bloomed — and absolutely stunning. The flower shop owner tells me to give it plenty of water — which is good because too much water is how I think I've been killing plants my whole non-gardening life.

And then another surprise: I find that I'm compelled to hothouse nurture this flowering plant, much like the way I felt about one of the plants that came home from the hospital with us when my daughter was born.

I water it, as advised, by soaking it in the kitchen sink. I move it by the sunniest window in the house during the day. When I come home, I place it on varying surfaces where it can show itself off. It's more work than I usually put into a house plant, but it seems to have my heart. I talk to it, telling it how beautiful it is. It bats its blossoms back at me; it positively prances. It becomes clearer that it is flourishing under my care and love. The care and love I'm aching to give — but can't — to my friend. I'm slathering it on the orchid. And it's beginning to show. On us both.

The Orchid

My pal is a plant person. As a landscape architect, she has the gift of gathering just the right living things and installing them so that they will thrive in just the right new setting.

Just as it seems I have done with this orchid.

Patience, I say to myself. Patience with not being able to do things for my dear friend in familiar ways. Patience in the knowledge that when she leaves the hospital and re-installs herself into a new place — like the living things she transplants — she will ultimately thrive like a strutting orchid.

February 2005

Stirring Thoughts on Morning Coffee

My morning must-have is an Ameri-misto — a four-layered brew made of three shots of decaffeinated espresso, boiling hot water, vanilla soy milk with an extra dollop of foam.

I've had to endure an enormous number of bad blends before I hit upon this perfect mix. I've knocked back many a latte, Americano and cappuccino and tinkered with two-percent, skim and even flavored milk until I settled on vanilla soy. It sweetens my mug without being sugary and the coffee provides just enough caffeine without giving me the shakes.

I can create this perfectly balanced blend at home — and do — but mostly I order it at a well-known coffee chain, sometimes forgoing lunch out to justify my $3-a-day addiction. But when I order it in public, my pleasure is offset by the fact that the name of my drink does not fall trippingly off the tongue. Lately I've become self-conscious — aware that my coffee colleagues may be thinking *just my luck that I'm lined up behind this persnickety X$@*&! ....* It's even more noticeable when I'm with my husband who orders *coffee, black*.

All of this comedy in the coffee shop has me wondering: Does my drink order say something about who I am? Are we a reflection of our favorite beverage?

If so, I'm in good company with my drink of distinction. James Bond liked his martini *shaken, not stirred*. Captain Picard of the Starship Enterprise sipped *Earl Grey, hot*. Thelonious Monk named an album after a particular way to down a drink: *straight, no chaser*.

Did these guys just pave the way for people like me to have it my way? Am I simply a victim of magnificent marketing?

Stirring Thoughts on Morning Coffee

Am I just hooked on the ritual of waking, caffeinating, working, sleeping, waking and caffeinating again?

Or is my coffee compulsion less about marketing and physical compulsion and more about psychology?

I think that what links me with others who go beyond *coffee, black* or a *soda* or *tea, please,* is that our orders are really recipes. We request drinks by providing instructions. We are particular — we like our drinks just right. Maybe we are a little bit controlling. Like the princess from the fairy tale who is sensitive enough to feel the pea underneath tons of thick mattresses. That's me: coffee royalty with a fine palate, one in need of the right taste complexity.

But I think my java jones goes beyond all of this: I think that it's about the satisfaction of performing a successful transaction. It is, after all, a business deal. There's a distinct beginning (my coffee order and its confirmation), middle (its preparation) and end (receipt and sip.) And unlike so much else going on around us, it is an exchange with an outcome I can count on.

If they could, I'd bet my movie spy, TV starship captain and dead jazz legend would drink to that.

March 2005

Art Appreciation

As my 17-year-old daughter and I were driving into the city a few months ago to visit liberal arts colleges, she noticed a city wall covered with graffiti and remarked on its beauty.

Her comments were not a surprise to me. She has been drawn to art all of her life — she has what we called at home, "an eye." But when I reminded her of this and asked why she wasn't considering art schools, she said, "Mom, I'm an art *appreciator,* not an art *maker.*"

It is an interesting distinction and I've been mulling it over ever since. There are people — like my daughter — who utilize music, for example, as a soundtrack for their daily activities: dressing and undressing, driving and falling asleep at night. They cover their bedroom walls with collages of magazine cuttings, stop to study a sculpture or abstract painting and note the loveliness of graffiti on a wall.

Though they surround themselves with the creative artifacts of human beings, art appreciators are not necessarily compelled to make art themselves. They prefer instead to allow the art to shift their mood, to bask in the emotions it stirs; to immerse themselves in the beauty or powerful messages.

This is what separates them from the artists. And until my daughter said so, I didn't recognize that it is also what distinguishes her from me.

I, too, am moved by the art I experience — but I am more fascinated by the process of making it. Artists see the world through a possibility lens, asking themselves: What if I took that idea and stretched it this way or that using sound or paint or clay or film or texture or landscape? They are insatiably curious and want to dig deeper to explore an idea or a feeling. Often they are not so good at letting these go. They get stalked by them. Sometimes haunted.

Making art is what some people do in response to living. It isn't enough just to comment on life, to share it in a conversation. That's wonderful, but for the artist, it isn't enough. Artists are interested in the act of expression. Making art is how they make sense of life.

Take me, for instance: I write for a living, but there is also the writing I do that is completely unattached to a paycheck — the kind that I do in journals, letters and on numerous scraps of paper. If several days go by and I have not had the chance to write something that comes from inside, I feel disconnected; anxious; nerve-racked; not myself.

Now let me interrupt myself here for just a moment to say that I believe, as the creativity guru Julia Cameron does, that virtually everyone is creative. Her numerous books on the subject remind us that people can be taught to bring out their creativity and even use this part of themselves in the business world.

But I'm talking about compulsion here: the overwhelming desire to respond to life by taking a Sharpie to a hard-bound journal or yellow pad; use horse hair dabbed in paint to spread onto textured cloth; to make words and images pop on a page, to plant seeds or transplant plants into a configuration to bring out the best in a piece of land, to visualize a handbag or blouse from piles of collected fabric.

The artist seeks alone time. Down time. She needs the quiet to absorb life's stimuli. Time to process events so that she can rearrange them in her imagination and respond in some form and then put something artful and tangible back out there for others to absorb. It's a dynamic thing. An in and an out. A back and a forth. I've often thought that artists seek something very much like a conversation with the Divine.

It's about being able to visualize something that isn't there yet. To imagine something different. And to do it by leaving one's own personal mark.

Art Appreciation

My daughter's comment stirred something else inside of me: It brought up a feeling that I've had ever since becoming a mother who is also a writer: That I have two children, but I've often felt that I've had to manage three. The need to make art can sometimes feel a lot like a needy child who is calling, tugging, cajoling. It wants to be addressed. It knocks. It nags. And when I ignore it or simply can't get to it, it can spin a tantrum inside of me. It comes out as yelling and screaming, and family can feel like Mom is mad at them. But really Mom is frustrated that she has not been able to get to a keyboard or a Sharpie pen. Because even though Mom loves her family with every inch of her heart, she answers to another powerful, albeit invisible, voice: the one inside.

June 2005

Black Pants

Some women friends and I were talking recently about how the hunt for the perfect pair of pants has changed since we became mothers. Where once we could fly into a favorite store, select a style we liked in our size and buzz out happily with them in hand, our success rates have been compromised by our post-delivery, ever-changing shapes.

Now we rely on microfiber, Lycra, support underwear, adjustable waistbands, and most importantly, our collection of black pants.

This is, apparently, the dark secret of women over 45. More practical than the little black dress and far more forgiving than blue jeans, black pants stand their ground as the one clothing item that women own most. In my own wardrobe, there are more black pants than underwear.

As we delved into the details, more confessions surfaced. We had purchased black pants for every occasion, mood and style phase — and often more than one pair. Among my own collection are black pants that are lined, linen, straight, stretch, capri, cigarette, cotton, gabardine, jean, palazzo, drawstring, sweat and bellbottom.

One friend joked that she'd thought about creating an art exhibit dedicated to her collection of black pants — hung clothesline style in some downtown gallery space. Another commented that when she's in a store trying on a pair in a different color, she'll often ask the saleswoman, "These are nice, but do you have them in black?"

How satisfying to learn that a black pant fixation is not mine alone. I've come to think of this realization as the moment I entered the *sisterhood of the black pants*.

Black Pants

You may have heard about the book by Ann Brashares titled *The Sisterhood of the Traveling Pants* — recently made into a movie. It's about a pair of blue jeans that fits four differently shaped teenage girls. The girls stay connected by sending the pants to one another one summer, along with letters detailing what happened to them when they were wearing them.

I won't bore you with what happened to me while wearing a pair of black pants — i.e., the last half decade of my life — but I did consult several women to see if I could get to the bottom of why we love our bottoms black.

"Black pants are like jeans," said one friend. "They go with everything. I've recently decided that I don't even look good in black, but I can't give up my addiction ...."

Said another, "Black pants are guaranteed to fit into any context. You can wear black pants to weddings, funerals, job interviews, dinners, concerts, plays, or even daytime brunches, lunches, or the office. I must say, if I have a 'first' time meeting or event scheduled, I will err on the side of caution and wear black."

The words *slimming, versatile, chic, cool, hip* and *urban* came up more than once.

Several said *Funny you should ask* as they had just been thinking they needed a new pair. Several others said they wish they had more in their closet.

Interestingly, the 30-somethings I checked with — and my teenage daughters — were neutral on the subject. They looked at me blankly as if I should go get myself a life. My theory: Their bodies haven't changed enough for them to have to think about it.

But why black? Why not brown, blue, gray or green?

One friend, an abstract painter, color consultant and owner of, at last count, about 14 pairs, provided a color commentary on the topic.

"Black is not a color," she said. "It doesn't reflect or absorb light — so it won't expand or add dimension to anything as, say, yellow would do." She explained that black is actually the absence of color, like "standing in a cornfield at 3 a.m., 10 miles from the nearest streetlight, with no headlight, flashlight or candlelight." You won't see a thing, she said. (My friend, who has hosted many art shows, chooses to wear black so as not to compete with her high-color abstract paintings.)

While we aren't wearing the same pants as the young girls from the sisterhood series, from far away we 40- and 50-somethings may very well look like we are. Bonding over clothing is truly one of the better experiences to come out of teenage girlhood. Wearing our "urban uniform," as one woman called it, bonds us older women, just as it does for Bridget, Carmen, Tibby and Lena. A bond that at midlife, women can still be pleased to share with teenage girls.

August 2005

Heat Wave

By now the baking temperatures and sweltering humidity are behind us and I, for one, am hugely relieved. On top of the heat wave that steamed the nation this summer, I was having one of my own.

A chemically induced one — in the form of hot flashes.

If you aren't familiar with these distracting little blazes, allow me to describe them: They come as sudden, intense sensations on your face and upper body and can leave you dizzy, weak, flushed or perspiring. Their appearance seems to have nothing to do with the temperature or whether you just exercised or showered. Sometimes you'll notice a moist upper lip, sometimes a soaked neck, and frequently, these are followed by a slight chill.

I think of myself as physically tough for a woman just under five foot two: I delivered both of my children without any drugs and I endured 30-some years of a vast array of premenstrual symptoms. Since I'm not in the habit of skulking from a challenge, I've read everything I can on how to manage these internal heat explosions. I exercise, take vitamins, drink decaf, limit alcohol and sugar, consume vegetables and fruit and soy products, and manage stress with good friends, yoga and a periodic massage.

But I swear, one more day of this double-helping heat wave was going to make me lose it.

Next to an increase in my personal laundry, the trying temperatures and unannounced beads of sweat forced another issue: Extreme discomfort can help you get quite clear about your likes, dislikes and limits.

I remember the moment when everything changed. It was the

middle of summer, during a long heat stretch when I was particularly busy with work projects. I arrived home, my back soaked just from a short commute from my office.

I'll spare you the details, but I said *no* to someone I know, someone I had been waiting for the right time to say *no* to, and ultimately, made her cry.

I'm not in the habit of doing this, but it felt right. I had claimed a boundary for myself. One that pushed us both to be more authentic with our time and our desires. I hope.

But this was only the beginning. Hormones and heat were partnering to help me make other, less dangerous, discoveries such as I really don't like stadium baseball games; chin-length hair is the right length for me, and expensive body lotion is really worth it.

I've heard people say that menopause is the passage into the wisdom years. That these flashes can offer insights and energy surges. That menopause is the center of a woman's life and that she can claim a second adulthood. Maybe this is true, but I've just been too damn overheated to ponder this for very long.

But I have wondered about the meaning of extreme heat and I have concluded that it slows us down and changes our chemistry.

I feel like I was liquefied this summer — melted down and re-hardened to discover the same me, only reconstituted. Some stuff moved to the top and some moved to the bottom and with these changes, I became a bit clearer. Clearer so that I can move on — drier — into the autumn of my life.

September 2005

Mission Statement # 24

Seven years ago, with an 11- and 8-year old as muses, I crafted a mission statement. It was December of 1999 and I called it "A Mother's Mission Statement for the Millennium."

There were 23 items in that statement, a document I refer to from time to time to see if I've stayed "on track."

Mostly the statements revolve around raising my children with good self-esteem:

I will encourage my children, support them, praise them, but honor their differences.

and with sound hygiene:

I will teach my children how to keep themselves clean, well fed, and healthy, but I will not hover over them until they are all of these things.

without spoiling them:

I will say no to my children if what they are asking is more than I can give at the time, and I will be okay about this.

and, at the same time, setting boundaries for myself with them as a working mother:

I will attend my children's plays, shows, competitions, graduations and other important events, but I will not beat myself up if, for some reason that is out of my control, I can't make it.

There are many turning-point moments for a mother — moments in which her child has a birthday and in the blink of a soppy eye, everything is different. I remember feeling misty on my oldest daughter's first day of kindergarten, at 10 (the first double digit age), 13 (bat mitzvah age) and 16 (driving age), but when she turned 18 just a few months ago, I felt more of a clang than a click.

She was positively exuberant on that day. She basked in this new number. She kept saying, "I'm an adult now, Mom. I can vote, I can rent an apartment — legally, there are things I don't have to tell you." (Oddly enough, she can do all these things, but she can't rent a car — she's got to be 25. Trust me, I checked.)

That was part of the big clang — her sense of entitlement to adulthood, when she is only just beginning to build support for that claim. (Twenty-one seems more like "true adult" to me, but I know this is easy for me to say now.)

I didn't dare take that moment from her, but I could not help but notice the blend of acceptance and melancholy. The acceptance was the feeling that the major part of my work with her was complete. That whatever else transpired between us, it would be small things. More financial support, sure (as college is right around the corner), and emotional support, absolutely, but I couldn't help but feel that as far as her foundation (and the architecture of her values) and certainly, the genes, these were already passed along. From here on it would be small saves rather than big ones.

A few days after her birthday, I went back to the manifesto to see if I could pick up any wisdom from my younger-mother self. And I read:

My children are on loan to me for a short while, shorter than they will live in the world independently (hopefully).

I was reminded that even back then, with two boisterous elementary school children in my house, in one of those calm, knowing, quiet moments of motherhood, I knew that my time to guide them and inspire them and make my impact was measured and would come to an end. That my contribution would be, over the long haul, very large and very small.

It got me thinking that even though I'm very much a product of my upbringing, I've still had many more years outside of my mother's house than in. Which makes me several more degrees a product of the life I've lived away from my family of origin. A result of the life I have lived on my own which began, of course, at 18. Like my daughter is about to do.

Which may account for the melancholy. From here on out, my daughter is very likely to morph into a slightly different version of herself. And I'll no longer be able to lay claim to it. When she began to drive, I began to see that there were going to be vistas and drivers that I wouldn't face with her or help her navigate. But now we're way beyond the neighborhood or the city and she's just been sprung on life's roadways. And I'm way behind her in the traffic jam of life, praying she's got cash for gas and a charged cell phone, and thinking about adding one more statement to the list:

Once they earn their wings, I will let them go with a glad heart.

May 2006

Longtime Friends

Some weeks ago I found myself in the middle of a long-lasting and solidly good frame of mind. I think of myself as an upbeat woman with my share of circumstantial, seasonal and hormonal ups and downs, but this stretch felt palpably different. I was content, cheery and, at moments, even joyful.

Because that period was so noticeable, I pondered the reasons. A few came right to mind: I was nearing the end of a multi-month challenging publishing assignment at work; nothing dramatically bad was happening with my children, husband or family members; and spring had sprung and we were having a noteworthy version. So I ascribed my fine mood to these factors and put the questioning aside.

Until it ended. Which then led me to wonder about one other factor. During those weeks, there had been an unusually large number of events with longtime friends. Several weekends had involved out-of-town buddies visiting me or me visiting them. I'm talking about old friends here — the ones that go back as far as early motherhood, college and even middle school.

I'm talking about the friends who have stuck around all these years. Through losing loved ones, sharing parenting issues, celebrating bat mitzvahs, monitoring pregnancies, standing up at weddings, tailgating at rock concerts, supporting professional twists and turns, standing by academic failures and successes, fights with parents and breakups with boyfriends.

These are the people who know your story. They know it so well that you don't need to spend time telling it (although it's always fun to retell some of it over long dinners.) Instead, the relationship has a unique benefit: It allows you to hang out in the present, which I discovered was a huge part of my happiness quotient.

What a rare thing it is to suspend for a while in real time. So many of our day-to-day exchanges are about discussing past acts or future ones. At work, it is *Can you meet on this day?* At the dry cleaner, it is *Were you able to get out the stain?* With the telephone company, it's *You think I owe what?* With our children it can be *You have soccer practice this afternoon, so take your cell phone.* So little of the content of daily backs and forths are about what is happening now, in this moment.

Which is what makes longtime friends so special. They are the ones who'll stop on that walk and look at the gigantic gold fish swimming in the pond. Or who will point out the unusual hues in the sky. Or who, on a night out, will tell you that you are particularly funny, or not funny, or that you should please stop snapping that chewing gum because they can't hear the concert. They are the ones where, over dinner, food is important, but not half as important as the conversation, and no one is rushing anywhere because this is where you all want to be. There's never a search for conversation, nor is there a need to fill in the quiet spaces.

This little revelation also provided me with some insight into handling my very social teenage daughters. I'm rather naggy on the subject of how their social lives get in the way of studying or household chores. How they put their friends first — before everything — mostly sleep and sometimes their own health. (*But Mom, I have to see Allie's brother play in the band at school to support Allie in spite of the fact that I've been out every other night this week!* Or Mom: *You don't understand — I have to help Stephanie move to another apartment — she needs my help!*) And I wag my finger, telling them that, yes, it's nice to be good to your friends, but not when there is so much else to do.

But I was reminded that good friends are stress busting. And we all need that — even adolescents. Perhaps I should focus on the fact that my daughters have and keep good friendships — a skill that will stay with them their entire lives.

Time to whip out the calendar and schedule some more of that present tense.

June 2006

High School Hopes, Revisited

As I was fanning myself with my program in an un-air-conditioned basketball gymnasium with hundreds of other moist parents and their capped and gowned 18-year-old graduates, I was remembering how just a few years ago, I wasn't sure this day would ever come.

Just three years ago, my daughter's early high school career looked somewhat ill-fated. What had been a consistent striving for high grades in middle school had begun to look to me like a whole lot of not striving at all.

And boy, did I sweat it. I worried that she was going to throw a perfectly good mind away. That she wouldn't graduate, wouldn't get into college and wouldn't be able to pursue her passions.

Oh, the pain of a mother's angst.

Yet, by junior year, her grades and her attitude about her studies slowly reversed. Grades climbed, awards and honorable mentions were earned, and she had her eye on — and got into — the college of her choice.

I share all this not for bragging rights — though I am very pleased — but because in between brow wipes, I found myself with a reversal of thinking of my own. All those years when she was struggling — and I, with her — she was gaining something that had eluded me. She had a brush with not doing her best. Now she knows what that feels like. And it will inform her from here on in.

Sitting in that gym, I couldn't help but recall what the college financial aid counselor said to us upon noting the discrepancy between my daughter's grade point average and her test scores. The counselor said that having had "an academic blip" in high school would probably be a benefit to her rather than a deficit. "She got her distracted days over early on," she said. When the super achiever kids descend onto campus and get their first taste of freedom, my daughter, who made freedom a priority, will be prepared. She'll probably do well as a result, because she's been there and back.

I'm finding this to be very ironic, really. I fretted so — practically panicked — when her grades started to slip. I got it in my head that she was ruining her life — that her entire future would slip away. But perspiring in that gym on graduation night provided me with drops of insight: Being on the other side of the grade point average has served her very well, indeed.

Some kids are competitive and goal driven. Other kids need to live life at the edges — to live experientially, slightly outside of the rules and with lots of freedom in order to learn. I was reminded that evening that my first-born is this second type: If she lives it, she knows it and then it sticks.

Like I was to that gym bleacher.

Our children have got to get there their own way. There really is no template, no direct route.

My daughter tells me that even when things got really bad grade-wise, she never worried about not graduating. She said she may have had to retake a course or resubmit a paper, but not graduating, no, this was never an option.

So what was my freaking out about? Was I simply looking into the face of my own worst fears? My own anxieties?

Probably. It seems to be an occupational hazard.

Fitting, then, that in a steamy gym on that June night, I experienced distinct and diametrically opposed sensations: I was delighted and outrageously uncomfortable. What a metaphor for marking our children's life cycle events: emotionally filling, physically challenging and always, always double-sided.

July 2006

Sensitivity in the Workplace

I have been working non-stop my entire adult life — except for a few short weeks after having children — but I have never stayed in a job more than two years.

And no, I have never been fired. It was me who did all of the leaving.

Since I'm nearing the two-year mark at the job I currently hold — a position that I have no intention to leave — I've been pondering this pattern. Have I had some sort of allergic reaction to the traditional office?

It hasn't been about finding the right career fit, because I've remained in the same field for more than 25 years. It hasn't been about being uprooted or finding the right geographic fit, because I've lived in the same town for that same length of time. It hasn't been about clashing personalities, because my bosses have been decent enough people. It's not even about the commute, because all of the places I have worked have been located no more than 15 miles from my home.

No, it's not that I don't like to work — at least no more than anyone else. Even when I wasn't working at a traditional workplace, I would return to freelance work life from a home office.

I've recently concluded that, up until now, this two-year limit has been about being a sensitive person. It is about the sounds, the smells, the light, the temperature, the wall coverings, the interruptions that come with cublicled offices.

Which is why I am writing this at my home office.

I've discovered that I fall into a group of folks known as highly sensitive people, or HSPs. We sensitive types enjoy our own company, are aware of other people's emotions, have a low tolerance for noise, glaring lights, strong odors, clutter or chaos and have an acute sense of a work environment.

For HSPs, who are usually off-the-charts brilliant (my assessment), traditional offices can be particularly challenging. Only about 30 percent of the working population are wired this way.

Since I've become aware of this characteristic, I've been looking around for signs of others. There's a woman I work with who brings in fresh-cut flowers for her work area. She occasionally burns scented candles and usually has a full pitcher of filtered water at her desk. Sometimes she'll play soft music from her computer terminal.

I've spotted another who brings oranges to work and leaves the peels out to fill her office with a wonderful citrus aroma.

A few other sensitive souls use air freshener in their cubicles or aromatic hand creams or even lay out primitive sculpture on built-in shelves.

I was heartened. We sensitives are an often misunderstood group, as we are not just using our very fine brains, we are also using our five senses — sometimes on overtime.

I've asked around and have noticed that those of us who share these traits tend to be artistic souls. In our off time, we are driven to the page, camera, music, kitchen or canvas to express ourselves or lose ourselves in beauty. People like us like to create stuff or be near people who do. It's how we make sense of life.

Making sense of life provides meaning to our lives, which gives us a reason to live. Shouldn't our work reflect who we are, as closely as it can? (Or it this question only a highly sensitive person would ask?)

Recognizing this about myself has taken a load off. I realize that I have spent much of my life chastising myself for these tendencies rather than celebrating them. I continue to look for ways to integrate pieces of my artistic soul into each day. And if I'm so damned creative, I ought to find a way.

August 2006

A Mother's Mark

Our recent family beach vacation was much like the many that came before, except that I was keenly aware that it could be our last.

Emily will be headed for college in a few weeks, and while it has always been part of the grand plan, I foresaw beyond a quieter house and a less hair-and-body-product strewn bathroom. From this point on, I thought, our family dynamic could change forever.

Just when it was getting so good.

Why is it that when we finally get a firm hold on the ways and means of family life — because we have come to understand or have learned patience — our children pick that moment to move into another emotional (or, in this case, physical) place? We get so little time to hang out on that piece of parent-child beachfront where the breezes, the temperature and the rhythm of the waves are just right.

Which is why at several moments during our days away, I found myself wondering: *What does it all mean, anyway? What is the purpose of family life?*

Several years ago, I pondered whether I could benefit as a parent from the progressive management techniques that my boss was using to motivate me. Could these be translated to encourage children? I read Dale Carnegie for his ideas about influencing people because, at the time, I wanted to positively influence my children.

Some of his ideas were interesting vis-à-vis family life. I particularly liked:

The only way to get the best of an argument is to avoid it.

Show respect for the other person's opinion. Never tell a person she is wrong.

If you are wrong, admit it quickly and emphatically.

Get the other person saying "yes, yes" immediately.

Let the other person feel that the idea is his.

Try honestly to see things from the other person's point of view.

But as my daughters have grown older, I do less motivational management and more facilitating. We are operating less like a traditional small business and more like a group of entrepreneurs.

I've decided that a traditional workplace model, with a manager impacting everyone else's output and quality of work, doesn't paint the proper portrait anymore. The goal is entirely different. Families are built for reconstruction. The parents I admire most have told me that you know you've done a good job raising your children if they grow up, evolve and, ultimately, leave.

This strikes me as a decent enough explanation for the purpose of family life. It's about constructing a firm and supportive structure — strong enough to take hits and the changes that life brings. But also recognizing that children ultimately become management. The goal then becomes everyone trying to be the best they can be while they simultaneously rely on — or have some faith in — the interdependence of family ties. Like a group of more equal businesspeople who gather to make their mark independently, and as a team.

My daughter will come home for a few days or weeks during academic breaks. She may even join us for short visits to see family out of town. But the chances for a long stretch of days with her may very well have come to an end. Her life is already brimming over with fullness — she's already got old friends, new roommates, a fresh course load, a new campus and a boyfriend. These are the elements of a full life with new priorities.

When she comes home for those breaks, she'll be doing most of the telling and we will be the listeners and her witnesses (with periodic support and critique, I'm sure).

Of course, the net will still be there — but her landings will be weightier and will shape not only who she is, but the ground beneath her feet. Like when you walk on the saturated part of the beachfront and leave behind an outline of your feet. You leave your own unique mark.

This last family trip reminded me that I'm officially done making my mark — a mother's mark — and that now it's Emily's turn. Only hers is slated for the world.

September 2006

She's Gone, Sort Of

Parents: When your child leaves for college, be easy on yourself as you have just arrived at a place that is reminiscent of coming home with a new baby. There you find yourself, bursting with emotion and relying on skills — mostly improvisational — that you didn't know you had.

The week my daughter left for college, I was a container of emotions waiting for the top to release. She was only 30 minutes away — when the traffic was flowing — but there were two emergency issues right from the start: 1) determining the frequency of contact once she was gone and 2) what my own reaction would be after we said goodbye.

For the question of how often we should be in contact, I did what any parent would do when she doesn't have any instructions: I relied on my own experience.

And what I know is that when I went to college, I got onto a plane and headed hundreds of miles away to return only at winter and spring break. Back then, before e-mail and cell phones, and the cost of long-distance calls kept my parents and me from talking more than weekly, and many times it went longer than that. It was a different time and a different cast of characters.

In the weeks prior to my older daughter leaving for college, I relied on "the script." I told her that I would wait to hear from her. I wouldn't call — that I'd give her the space and time she needed to get used to her new surroundings.

(Isn't it funny how we default to how-it-was-when-we were-our-children's-age even though we aren't our parents and our children aren't us?)

And it worked, for 24 hours.

After a day passed, I had to hear her voice just to know that she was okay, even though she's always been extremely independent and self-sufficient. I called and when she picked up, she said, "Hi, Mom. Why didn't you call sooner?"

Two days after she settled into school, she was back at home for dinner. And then, two days after that, with her first classes behind her, she asked if her dad and I could meet her for dinner at her favorite Thai restaurant. And then, two days after that, she showed up at our door to collect some things from her room.

We saw her three times that first week. Who would have figured?

Another thing I would not have figured: I expected to dissolve into tears after our first goodbye. I had even prepared for it, asking my mother-in-law — an organizational wizard — to join us on moving day so that she could direct where things should go and I could allow myself the luxury of feeling what the day brought. (I suppose it was a feeble attempt on my part to engage in a personal college goodbye ritual.)

Oddly, my eyes stayed dry and my mind was on task. It was a day for traveling stairs, meeting her roommates and buying gadgets at large discount warehouses.

That evening, on the ride home, I thought the water would fall, but it didn't.

But nature won't let us get away long without acknowledging big life passages such as this one. My moment came, biblically, on the seventh day. In a rare moment alone in the house, when everything was really quiet, it finally hit me. She was gone (sort of), and I had myself a good, hearty sob.

Though not for long, as my younger daughter's key turned in the front door and she bounded in, deposited her backpack and muddy running shoes in the front hall, headed to the kitchen for a snack and then to her computer for some quick IM-ing before homework. I threw cold water on my face, popped open her door, said hello, asked if she needed anything, and without even looking up, she said no. Ordinarily, she would have received one of my miffed looks, as she knows that her backpack needs to come to her room and she can't bring food up there — but that day, after processing one daughter's departure, I was just happy that there was still one left in the house. I've got four more years before I go through this goodbye ritual again. But I'll probably have to start from scratch because she's a different person, and, clearly, so am I.

October 2006

The Barish family in the fall of 2006.
From left: Ellen, Emily (18), Jenny Rose (15), and David.

After Words

We never really know how things are going when we are in the midst of mothering. It's only by our intuition — or comparing then to now — that we ever get the slightest bit of information.

But when our emotions fuzz up our gut feeling, it's good to have some tangible evidence of "then" so that we can compare it to the present. The "big picture" signal is so easy to lose. Which is at least one argument for saving our children's artwork, taking lots of snap shots and, of course, for writing things down.

Now that I have a daughter in college and another in high school, I am beginning to see signs that my efforts have amounted to something. And those somethings are living, breathing creatures who will, hopefully, contribute to the world.

But I must say a word or two about other mothers, especially the ones who are a few steps farther down the mothering path than me. I am so blessed to have had them in my life. I thank them for their wisdom and compassion and for taking time from their overloaded lives when I sought them out. To these women, my deepest appreciation. They listened well and gave me what I needed most, which may not have seemed like much to them at the time: a knowing nod; some encouraging words; a long, deep sigh. Responses that I dearly hope I gave to that young mother at work who is 10 years behind me in her mothering journey.

Even though the intense early years of mothering are over for me, I plan on keeping these women at close range. I will continue to look to them for ideas about the next stage. I see them traveling, enrolling in cooking school, taking adult education classes, forming women's groups or going on writing, spiritual or biking retreats.

They are entering the next part of their lives with gusto.

I urge you to find other mothers, especially ones with children older than yours, whom you admire for one reason or another who are happy to share what they've learned. Observe them for reminders that there are so many choices for a woman after her children move out and into adulthood, even though a woman's children will always be a huge part of who she is.

January 2007

About the Author

Barish's essays have been syndicated by Tribune Media Services International and have appeared in the *Chicago Tribune, North Shore Magazine* and have aired on WBEZ-Chicago Public Radio. As a freelance writer and editor, she has covered health and parenting topics for the *Chicago Tribune, Newsweek, Self* and *Chicago Parent.* Barish has taught writing at Chicago-area colleges, including Northwestern University, where she earned a master's degree in journalism from the Medill School. She is a freelance writer and editor and lives near Chicago with her husband and youngest of two daughters. To read more of Barish's columns, go to www.ellenblumbarish.com.

About the Publisher

Adams Street Publishing is a Toledo, Ohio-based, family-owned media company that publishes the monthly parenting magazines *Toledo Area Parent News* and *Ann Arbor Family Press*, in addition to Northwest Ohio's only award-winning alternative-weekly newspaper, the *Toledo City Paper*. For more information about the company, go to www.adamsstreetpublishing.com.